GREAT AIRCRAFT OF WORLD WAR II

SUPERMARINE SPITFIRE

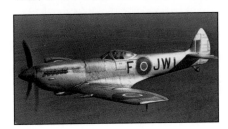

GREAT AIRCRAFT OF WORLD WAR II
SUPERMARINE SPITFIRE
AN ILLUSTRATED GUIDE SHOWN IN OVER 100 IMAGES

ALFRED PRICE

LORENZ BOOKS

This edition is published by Lorenz Books,
an imprint of Anness Publishing Ltd,
108 Great Russell Street,
London WC1B 3NA;
info@anness.com

www.lorenzbooks.com; www.annesspublishing.com

Anness Publishing has a new picture agency outlet for images for publishing, promotions
or advertising. Please visit our website www.practicalpictures.com for more information.

© Anness Publishing Ltd 2015

Publisher: Joanna Lorenz
Senior Editor: Felicity Forster
Production Controller: Pirong Wang

PUBLISHER'S NOTE
Although the advice and information in this book are believed to be accurate
and true at the time of going to press, neither the authors nor the publisher can
accept any legal responsibility or liability for any errors or omissions that may have
been made nor for any inaccuracies nor for any loss, harm or injury that
comes about from following instructions or advice in this book.

Page 1: **After the war, Spitfires served in several second-line units. This Mark XVI operated with the Central Gunnery School.**
Page 2: **A Spitfire VII, the high-altitude interceptor version of the famous fighter.**
Page 3: **A Spitfire Mark II of No. 411 (Canadian) Squadron, at Digby in Lincolnshire in 1941.**
Below: **The 600th production Spitfire during its testing in April 1940.**

CONTENTS

INTRODUCTION

Rheine, western Germany, 13.35 hours, 29 December 1944

A dozen Spitfires of No. 411 (Canadian) Squadron, flying in three separate four-plane sections, traced lazy patterns in the sky high above the important Luftwaffe airfield. Leading Yellow Section was Flight Lieutenant Dick Audet, a 22-year old of French extraction flying his 53rd operational sortie. During the previous months he had carried out numerous bombing and strafing attacks on ground targets, but he had yet to encounter enemy aircraft in the air.

The Spitfires' mission was to engage German aircraft taking off from the airfield or on the landing approach to it. Suddenly Audet caught sight of a dozen hostile fighters in loose formation far below. He gave a clipped radio call to inform his commander of the enemy presence and to say that he was about to engage. Then Audet led his Section into a steep diving turn, moving his force as rapidly as possible into a firing position behind the German planes. It was to be a classic fighter 'bounce', with no quarter asked or given. In his combat report Audet later wrote:

"The enemy were four Messerschmitt 109s and eight Focke Wulf 190s, flying line astern. I attacked an Me 109, the last aircraft in the formation. At 200 yards I opened fire and saw strikes all over the fuselage and wing roots. The 109 burst into flames and trailed black smoke.

"I now went around in a defensive circle until I spotted an FW 190. I attacked from 250 yards down to 100 yards and from 30 degrees from line astern.

Below: Flight Lieutenant Dick Audet scored five victories during his first encounter with enemy aircraft, on 29 December 1944.
Right: Spitfire Mark IXs of Audet's unit, No. 411 Squadron, warming their engines at their base at Heesch in Holland, before a mission.

saw strikes all over the cockpit and to the rear of the fuselage. It burst into flames. I saw the pilot slumped in his cockpit.

"Ahead was a 109 going down in a slight dive. It pulled up sharply into a climb, and the cockpit canopy flew off. I gave a short burst at about 300 yards and the aircraft whipped down in a dive. The pilot attempted to bail out, but his chute ripped to shreds. I saw the 109 hit the ground and smash into flaming pieces.

"I next spotted an FW 190 being pursued by a Spitfire pursued in turn by an FW 190. I called this pilot – one of my Yellow Section – to break, and attacked the 109 from the rear. We went down in a steep dive. I opened fire at 250 yards and it burst into flames. I saw it go into the ground and burn.

"Several minutes later, while attempting to re-form my section, I spotted an FW 190 at about 3000 feet. I dived on him and he turned into me from the right. He then flipped around in a left-hand turn, and attempted a head-on attack. I slowed down to wait for him to fly into range. At about 200 yards I gave a short burst. I could not see any strikes but he flicked violently and continued to do so until he crashed."

Within 10 minutes Dick Audet had shot down five enemy aircraft, to gain for himself the coveted status of fighter ace. Other pilots in the squadron witnessed the feat, and it would later be confirmed by analysis of his combat camera film. During the action, other pilots in Audet's squadron destroyed three more enemy fighters.

Although the Spitfire had been in service for six years, the versions in service at the end of 1944 were still formidable fighting machines. Yet, paradoxically, the fighter was designed for a purpose quite different from that flown by Dick Audet on that December afternoon. The Spitfire was designed solely as an air defence interceptor, to engage and destroy enemy bombers attempting to attack targets in the British Isles. The Spitfire fulfilled that task brilliantly, and was equally effective in hunting down enemy fighters over their own territory. In those and a dozen other roles, the sleek-lined little fighter illustrated its versatility.

SUPERMARINE SPITFIRE VB

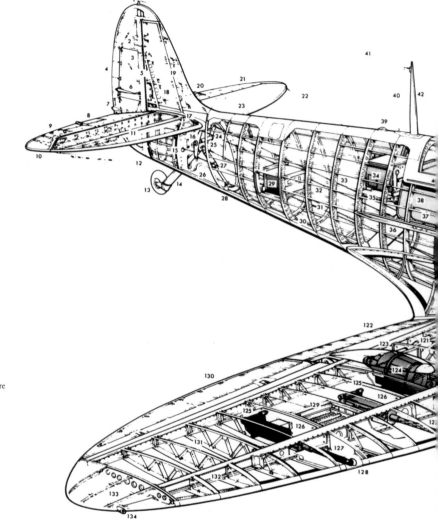

1 Aerial stub attachment
2 Rudder upper hinge
3 Fabric-covered rudder
4 Rudder tab
5 Sternpost
6 Rudder tab hinge
7 Rear navigation light
8 Starboard elevator tab
9 Starboard elevator structure
10 Elevator balance
11 Tailplane front spar
12 IFF aerial
13 Castoring non-retractable tailwheel
14 Tailwheel strut
15 Fuselage double frame
16 Elevator control lever
17 Tailplane spar/fuselage attachment
18 Fin rear spar (fuselage frame extension)
19 Fin front spar (fuselage frame extension)
20 Port elevator tab hinge
21 Port elevator
22 IFF aerial
23 Port tailplane
24 Rudder control lever
25 Cross shaft
26 Tailwheel oleo access place
27 Tailwheel oleo shock-absorber
28 Fuselage angled frame
29 Battery compartment
30 Lower longeron
31 Elevator control cables
32 Fuselage construction
33 Rudder control cables
34 Radio compartment
35 Radio support tray

36 Flare chute
37 Oxygen bottle
38 Auxiliary long-range fuel tank (29 gallon/132 litre)
39 Dorsal formation light
40 Aerial lead-in
41 HF aerial
42 Aerial mast
43 Cockpit aft glazing
44 Voltage regulator
45 Canopy track
46 Structural bulkhead

47 Headrest
48 Plexiglass canopy
49 Rear-view mirror
50 Entry flap (port)
51 Air bottles (alternative rear fuselage stowage)
52 Sutton harness
53 Pilot's seat (moulded Bakelite)
54 Datum longeron
55 Seat support frame
56 Wingroot fillet
57 Seat adjustment lever

58 Rudder pedal frame
59 Elevator control connecting tube
60 Control column spade grip
61 Trim wheel
62 Reflector gunsight
63 External windscreen armour
64 Instrument panel
65 Main fuselage fuel tank (48 gallon/218 litre)
66 Fuel tank/longeron attachment fittings

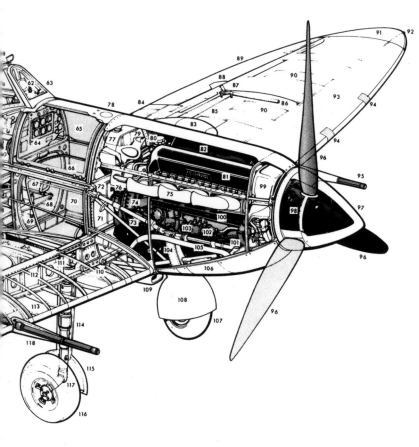

101 Engine anti-vibration
    mounting pad
102 Engine accessories
103 Engine bearers
104 Main engine support member
105 Coolant pipe
106 Exposed oil tank
107 Port mainwheel
108 Mainwheel fairing
109 Carburettor air intake
110 Stub/spar attachment
111 Mainwheel leg pivot point
112 Main spar
113 Leading-edge ribs (diagonals
    deleted for clarity)
114 Mainwheel leg shock-absorber
115 Mainwheel fairing
116 Starboard mainwheel
117 Angled axle
118 Cannon barrel support fairing
119 Spar cut-out
120 Mainwheel well
121 Gun heating pipe
122 Flap structure
123 Cannon wing fairing
124 Cannon magazine drum
    (120 rounds)
125 Machine-gun support brackets
126 Gun access panels
127 .303in machine-gun barrels
128 Machine-gun ports
129 Ammunition boxes (350rpg)
130 Starboard aileron construction
131 Wing ribs
132 Single-tube outer spar section
133 Wingtip structure
134 Starboard navigation light

57 Rudder pedals
58 Rudder bar
59 King post
70 Fuselage lower fuel tank
    (37 gallon/168 litre)
71 Firewall/bulkhead
72 Engine bearer attachment
73 Steel tube bearers
74 Magneto
75 'Fishtail'/exhaust manifold
76 Gun heating 'intensifier'
77 Hydraulic tank

78 Fuel filler cap
79 Air compressor intake
80 Air compressor
81 Rolls-Royce Merlin 45 engine
82 Coolant piping
83 Port cannon wing fairing
84 Flaps
85 Aileron control cables
86 Aileron push tube
87 Bellcrank
88 Aileron hinge
89 Port aileron

90 Machine-gun access panels
91 Port wingtip
92 Port navigation light
93 Leading-edge skinning
94 Machine-gun ports (protected)
95 20mm cannon muzzle
96 Three-blade constant-speed
    propeller
97 Spinner
98 Propeller hub
99 Coolant tank
100 Cowling fastening

A FIGHTER IS BORN

The story of the Spitfire began almost exactly ten years before Dick Audet's famous action, in December 1934. Then, at the Supermarine Aviation Company's works at Southampton, Reginald Mitchell and his team finalized the layout of their new high-speed fighter for the RAF.

Mitchell had already established his name as a highly successful designer of racing floatplanes for the Schneider Trophy competition. One of his designs – the Supermarine S.5 – had won that international contest in 1927. The S.6 won it two years later in 1929. After another two-year gap the Supermarine S.6B won the trophy outright for Britain in 1931, and later went on to raise the World Air Speed record to 407mph (655km/hr).

These had been magnificent achievements but, in the nature of things, the market for high-speed racing seaplanes was extremely limited. The Supermarine company's main 'bread and butter' products were its big Southampton and Scapa flying boats which now equipped seven RAF maritime patrol squadrons.

In 1934, the fastest fighter type in the Royal Air Force was the Hawker Fury, which had a maximum speed of 207mph at 14,000ft (333km/hr at 4,270m). At that time Air Vice Marshal Hugh Dowding held the post of Air Member for Supply and Research, and was responsible for issuing to manufacturers the specifications for new aircraft required for the Royal Air Force. Dowding was an exceptionally farsighted innovator, what we would now call a 'technocrat'. He saw the vital need for a new fighter to bridge the huge gap in

performance between the Schneider Trophy racers and the biplanes that were then in service.

The early 1930s saw rapid advances in aviation technology. The Schneider Trophy racing seaplanes had demonstrated the performance advantages of using highly supercharged engines, streamlined all-metal airframes and the monoplane wing layout. These features were also being incorporated into the latest land planes, together with wing flaps to reduce the landing speeds, and retractable undercarriages.

■ MITCHELL'S FIRST FIGHTER ■

In February 1934, Reginald Mitchell's first fighter design appeared, the Supermarine Type 224. The aircraft took part in the competition to select a new fighter type for the Royal Air Force. Although it

Opposite: Production of wings at Woolston, early in 1939.

THE SCHNEIDER TROPHY AND THE SPITFIRE

The Supermarine S.6B, Reginald Mitchell's final racing floatplane design, gained the Schneider Trophy outright for Great Britain in 1931. Later that year, it raised the world absolute speed record to 407mph (655km/hr).

One frequently repeated myth about the Spitfire is that it was 'developed from' the Supermarine S.6B. This is simply not true. Certainly Mitchell learned a lot about high-speed flight from his work on the floatplanes, but that is quite different from saying that the Spitfire was 'developed from' them. In fact, the two aircraft were quite different designs, intended for quite different roles. There was not a single component of any significance in the Spitfire that resembled its counterpart in the racing seaplane.

Type Single-seat racing floatplane
Power plant One Rolls-Royce 'R' engine developing 2,350hp
Dimensions Span 30ft 0in (9.14m); length 28ft 10in (8.79m)
Weight Maximum loaded weight 6,086lb (2760kg)
Performance Maximum speed 407mph at 245ft (655km/hr at 75m), a world record

Right: The Supermarine S.6B racing floatplane won the coveted Schneider Trophy outright for Great Britain in 1931. Later that year, it captured the world absolute speed record at 407mph (655km/hr).

SUPERMARINE TYPE 224

REGINAL MITCHELL'S FIRST FIGHTER DESIGN

This single-seat interceptor fighter used a novel type of evaporative cooling for the engine, employing a steam condenser built into the leading edge of each wing. The system gave continual trouble and would probably have precluded the fighter being ordered for the RAF even if its performance had been more impressive.

Type Single-seat interceptor fighter
Armament Four Vickers .303in (7.7mm) machine-guns synchronized to fire through the propeller arc
Power plant One Rolls-Royce Goshawk developing 680hp
Dimensions Span 45ft 10in (13.97m); length 29ft 5¼in (8.97m)

Weight Maximum loaded weight 4,743lb (2,151kg)
Performance Maximum speed 228mph at 15,000ft (367km/hr at 4,575m); time to climb to 15,000ft, 9½ minutes

Above: The Supermarine Type 224, Reginald Mitchell's unsuccessful first attempt at designing a fighter aircraft.

Right: The Hawker Fury, the fastest fighter type in the RAF in 1934, had a maximum speed of 207mph (333km/hr).

was a monoplane design of all-metal construction, the fighter had a fixed undercarriage and a rather clumsy appearance. The Type 224 proved a flop. Its maximum speed was only 228mph (367km/hr) and it took 9½ minutes to reach 15,000ft (4,575m). The unusual system of evaporative cooling for the engine, using a steam condenser mounted along the leading edge of each wing, gave continual trouble. The winner of the competition, the Gloster entrant later named the Gladiator, had a maximum speed of 242mph (390km/hr) and it climbed to 15,000ft in 6½ minutes. One thing was clear: a good biplane design would outperform an over-conservative monoplane design.

Having learned that painful lesson, Reginald Mitchell persuaded the company to allow him to design a smaller, lighter and more streamlined fighter. This time he would use the new 1,000 horsepower V-12 engine, later named the Merlin, which was then under test at the Rolls-Royce company in Derby. When Air Vice Marshal Dowding saw details of the proposed new fighter, he gave it his full support and issued an official Royal Air Force specification so that the government would meet most of the cost of building a prototype.

The new fighter made its maiden flight on 5 March 1936, with Chief Test Pilot 'Mutt' Summers at the controls. This was an altogether more effective machine than its predecessor and it aroused immediate interest. Not long afterwards, the Air Ministry allocated a name to the new fighter – 'Spitfire'. Had the decision been left to its designer, the aircraft would certainly have been named differently. When Mitchell learned of the official choice of name, he was heard to comment

FASTEST FIGHTER

"It is claimed – and the claim seems indisputable – that the Spitfire is the fastest military aeroplane in the world. It is surprisingly small and light for a machine of its calibre (the structural weight is said to have been brought down to a level never before attained in the single-seat fighter class), and its speed and manoeuvrability are something to marvel at.

Tight turns were made at high speed after dives, and the control at low speeds was amply demonstrated. The demonstration was cramped by low clouds, but after the main flying display the machine was taken up again and gave one of the smoothest displays of high-speed aerobatics ever seen in this country."

FLIGHT MAGAZINE, 3 JULY 1936

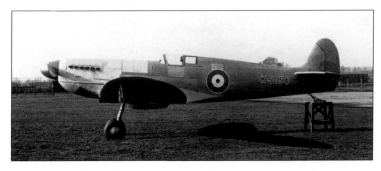

Above: The prototype Supermarine F. 37/34, serial number K 5054, pictured at Eastleigh shortly before its maiden flight. The metal parts of the aircraft were unpainted, the aircraft carried no armament and the undercarriage was locked in the down position.

'It's the sort of bloody-silly name they would give it!"

During flight tests, the new fighter attained a maximum speed of 349mph at 16,800ft (562km/hr at 5,122m), and in the climb it reached 30,000ft (9,145m) in 17 minutes. Not only was it the fastest fighter in existence, but it was also one of the most heavily armed, for it was designed to carry eight Browning .303in (7.7mm) machine-guns in the wings.

■ LARGE ORDER ■

The Spitfire became available at exactly the right time for the Royal Air Force. In Germany the recently re-formed Luftwaffe was building up its strength rapidly. Its new monoplane fighter type, the Messerschmitt 109, was on the point of entering large-scale production. To meet the mounting threat, in June 1936 the British Government signed a contract for 310 Spitfires.

The Spitfire made its first public appearance on 18 June 1936, during a press day held at Eastleigh to show aircraft made by the Supermarine and Vickers companies. Other aircraft taking part included a Walrus amphibian (another of Mitchell's designs) and the prototype Wellington bomber. With press photographers eagerly snapping away, Jeffrey Quill started the

Spitfire's engine and taxied to one end of the grass runway. Then he pushed open the throttle to begin his take-off run and the lightly loaded aircraft rapidly gained speed. Before getting airborne the pilot made a brief scan of his instruments, and noticed the needle of the oil pressure gauge suddenly drop to zero. That left him in an unenviable position. He had no room to stop before reaching the airfield boundary, and on the other side of it lay the sprawling buildings of the Southern Railway Company's locomotive works. Fearing that the engine might seize up at any moment, the pilot eased the aircraft into the air and reduced power to the minimum necessary

to hold it there. Then he took it round in a shallow turn, aiming to get it back to the airfield as soon as possible. The engine maintained its healthy roar, but as Quill lined up for the landing, he saw he was a little too low. He eased open the throttle for one last burst of power, the engine responded, and he made a safe landing. Examination of the engine revealed that an oil pipe

PROTOTYPE SPITFIRE

Type Single-seat interceptor fighter
Armament Eight .303in (7.7mm) Browning machine-guns with 350 rounds per gun
Power plant One Rolls-Royce Merlin Type C liquid cooled V-12 engine with single-speed supercharger developing 990hp
Dimensions Span 40ft (12.1m); length 29ft 11in (9.17m)
Weight Maximum loaded 5,395lb (2,446kg)
Performance Maximum speed 349mph at 16,800ft (562km/hr at 5,122m); service ceiling 35,400ft (10,790m)

Above: Close to disaster! Jeffrey Quill taking off in the prototype Spitfire during the press day at Eastleigh on 18 June 1936. A few seconds before this photograph was taken, when it was too late to abort the take-off, an oil pipe had come adrift. In the

background is the sprawling Southern Railway works over which the aircraft had to pass before it returned to the airfield. By skilful flying, Quill took the fighter in a wide circuit and landed before the engine seized. Had the prototype been lost that day, it is

possible that the RAF might have cancelled its order, in which case the Spitfire would not have gone into production.
Below left: The Supermarine works at Woolston on the outskirts of Southampton, close beside the River Itchen.

had come adrift, allowing the lubrication system to run dry. The engine was changed and sent to Rolls-Royce for examination, but it had suffered remarkably little damage from this treatment.

Had the prototype been lost during its first air display, the consequences to

the nation hardly bear thinking about. Only the one Spitfire existed, and it had not completed its initial performance trials with the Royal Air Force. If it had crashed, the Royal Air Force would probably have cancelled the contract and ordered other types of fighter instead. That would have had a

disastrous effect on the capability of Fighter Command during the Battle of Britain, four years later.

Thanks to Jeffrey Quill's skilful flying however, there had been no crash. Five days later the Spitfire resumed flying with a new engine. On 27 June, Flight Lieutenant Hugh Edwardes-Jones demonstrated the aircraft before a large crowd at the Royal Air Force Pageant at Hendon. Two days later, 'Mutt' Summers flew it at the Society of British Aircraft Constructors' air display at Hatfield. The demonstrations aroused enormous public interest in the fighter and drew lyrical descriptions in the press.

■ ON DISPLAY ■

The prototype completed its initial service trials at Martlesham Heath in July 1936, and returned to Eastleigh for modification. The fighter received a newer version of the Merlin, giving lightly greater power, and eight machine-guns were fitted in the wings.

Not all aspects of the Spitfire's flight trials went off smoothly. One of the most serious problems was that the fighter's guns did not work reliably at high altitude. During the initial firing trials in March 1937, all eight guns fired perfectly at 4,000ft (1,220m). It was a different story a few days later, when an RAF pilot climbed the Spitfire to 32,000ft (9,755m) over the North Sea for the first high-altitude firing. It nearly ended in tragedy. One gun fired 171 rounds before it failed, another fired 8 rounds, one fired 4 rounds, and the remaining five guns failed to fire at all. That was bad enough, but when the Spitfire touched down at Martlesham Heath after the test, the shock of the landing released the previously frozen-up breech blocks. Three of the weapons loosed off a round in the general direction of Felixstowe, fortunately without hitting anyone.

"... the Spitfires will be useless as fighting aircraft ..."

During the next 18 months, Supermarine engineers tried various schemes to solve the problem of gun freezing, using hot air ducted from the aircraft's glycol radiator. Yet the guns were still not functioning reliably in July 1938 when the first production Spitfires were delivered to the Royal Air Force. This led the Chief of the Air Staff, Marshal of the Royal Air Force Sir Cyril Newall, to comment during a secret meeting of the Air Council: "If the guns will

"MY GOD, IT'S MADE OF TIN!"

Whenever the prototype Spitfire landed away from its base, it was the subject of great interest. At that time, most airframes comprised a wood or light metal framework with a covering of linen fabric. The streamlined all-metal monoplane Spitfire with its enclosed cockpit and retractable undercarriage made every other aircraft in the Royal Air Force look positively prehistoric!

During a test flight in December 1936, Jeffrey Quill ran short of fuel, and he landed the Spitfire at the fighter airfield at Tangmere near Chichester. As he taxied in, a crowd of curious RAF ground crewmen gathered to meet it. Then, Quill recalled: "I taxied to a standstill and shut down, and could hear a tapping sound rather like raindrops hitting the aircraft. But it was a clear day. I checked I had shut everything down, but the tapping sound continued. Then as I climbed out I saw the reason. Several mechanics were standing around the rear fuselage, tapping it with their knuckles disbelievingly. 'My God,' one of them exclaimed, 'It's made of tin!'"

not fire at heights at which the Spitfires are likely to encounter enemy bombers, the Spitfires will be useless as fighting aircraft ..."

It took until October 1938 to resolve the problem. Then, on the 14th, a service pilot took the prototype to high altitude and fired off the entire contents of the ammunition boxes without a single stoppage. The gun-heating modification was then incorporated in all Spitfires on the production line.

During the test programme, the prototype Spitfire survived two serious accidents. During the first, in March 1937, it made an emergency wheels-up landing following an engine failure; and almost exactly a year later it suffered an undercarriage collapse on landing, following a fatigue fracture of one of the main wheel legs. On both occasions, the aircraft resumed flying after repairs. By the end of 1938, production Spitfires

were emerging from the assembly hangar at Eastleigh at an encouraging rate, and the test programme of the prototype was complete. In those days there were no sentimental ideas about preserving historic aircraft, and the first Spitfire went to Farnborough for use as a 'hack' aircraft. On 4 September 1939, the day after Britain entered the Second World War, the aircraft suffered serious damage in a fatal landing accident. The venerable aircraft could have been repaired, but since there was no further use for it, the machine was scrapped.

The prototype Spitfire had cost the public purse a mere £15,776. Rarely has the money of British taxpayers been better spent.

Below: The prototype Spitfire wearing drab military camouflage, in 1938. The muzzles of the two outer machine-guns can be seen protruding from the wing.

Having gained the initial order for 310 Spitfires, the Supermarine I Company found that fulfilling the contract was more difficult than expected. Previously the company had built small batches of flying boats for the Royal Air Force, and its work force numbered only about 500. The new all-metal fighter required specialized manufacturing techniques, and at a time when the aircraft industry was expanding, it was difficult to recruit workers with the necessary skills. As a result, there were delays in getting the fighter into production.

In August 1938, 29 months after the maiden flight of the prototype, No. 19 Squadron at Duxford received the first Spitfires. It took until December for the unit to get its full complement of aircraft, then other squadrons began to re-equip with the type. By this time Hugh Dowding had been promoted to Air Chief Marshal and held the post of Commander-in-Chief RAF Fighter Command. By a quirk of history, the man who had done so much to bring the Spitfire into being was now to direct these fighters into action.

When Great Britain declared war on Germany in September 1939, Royal Air Force Fighter Command possessed 187 Spitfires in front-line units. Nos. 19, 41, 54, 65, 66, 72, 74, 602, 603 and 611 Squadrons were fully equipped with Spitfires and No. 609 Squadron was in the process of converting to the type.

Spitfires first saw action on 6 September 1939, during the so-called 'Battle of Barking Creek'. Because of a technical fault at the radar station at Canewdon in Essex, aircraft flying west of the station appeared on the screen as if their position was east of the radar (i.e. in the direction from which a German raiding force heading for London would make

Main left: The cockpit of an early production Spitfire I.

Inset left: Spitfires of No. 19 Squadron practising formation flying, early in 1939.

SPITFIRE I

Type Single-seat interceptor fighter

Armament Eight Browning .303in (7.7mm) machine-guns with 350 rounds per gun

Power plant One Rolls-Royce Merlin II liquid cooled V-12 engine with single-speed supercharger developing 1,030 horsepower

Dimensions Span 36ft 10in (10.98m); length 29ft 11in (9.11m)

Weight Maximum loaded weight 5,819lb (2,639kg)

Performance Maximum speed 362mph at 18,500ft (583km/hr at 5,640m); service ceiling 31,900ft (9,725m)

Top: Spitfires and Hurricanes from several squadrons lined up at Digby in Lincolnshire. The aircaft had assembled there prior to a massed flypast over cities in the Midlands, to mark Empire Air Day on 20 May 1939. (No. 72 Squadron Archive)

Above and overleaf: The 600th production Spitfire during its testing in April 1940. During the Battle of Britain, this aircraft served with No. 64 Squadron.

Spitfires first saw action on 6 September 1939, during the so-called 'Battle of Barking Creek'

its approach). The operators at Canev don reported 20 unidentified aircra heading towards London from the eas and to meet the threat, several fight squadrons were scrambled. With

For the next hour, complete and utter chaos reigned over the Thames estuary

minutes the 'incoming formation being tracked on the radar, all of the now designated as 'hostile', increase to 12. Despite the poor weather, looked as if the Luftwaffe was about launch its expected onslaught on the capital. The defences came to full ale

A GERMAN PILOT'S OPINION OF THE SPITFIRE

Below: Spitfires in captivity. By the beginning of the Battle of Britain, the Germans had captured four Spitfires in flying or repairable condition.
Bottom: A captured Spitfire painted in bogus British markings and used in propaganda photographs.

"I was able to fly a captured Spitfire at Jever. My first impression was that it had a beautiful engine. It purred. The engine of the Messerschmitt 109 was very loud. Also the Spitfire was easier to fly, and to land, than the Me 109. The 109 was unforgiving of any inattention. I felt familiar with the Spitfire from the very start. That was my first and lasting impression. But with my experience with the 109, I personally would not have

traded it for a Spitfire. I had the impression, though I did not fly the Spitfire long enough to prove it, that the 109 was the faster, especially in the dive. Also, I think the pilot's view was better from the 109. In the Spitfire one flew further back, a bit more over the wing."

OBERLEUTNANT HANS SCHLOLLER-HALDY,
MESSERSCHMITT 109 PILOT,
FIGHTER GESCHWADER 54

soon afterwards an anti-aircraft
battery opened fire at 'twin-
engined bombers' passing overhead.
Shortly after that, the leader of a
Spitfire squadron broadcast a 'Tally
Ho!' call, to indicate that he had
enemy planes in sight and was about
to engage. For the next hour, complete
and utter chaos reigned over the
Thames Estuary. Squadrons of fighters
cruised between the banks of cloud,
seeking enemy planes but finding only
friendly ones. There were several brief
fire fights, each one broken off when it
became evident that the 'opponents'
were 'friendlies'. In the end, shortage of

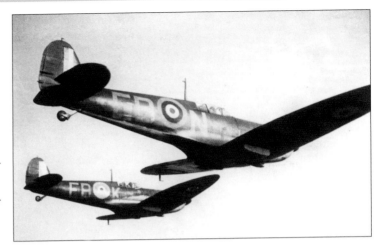

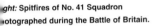

Right: Spitfires of No. 41 Squadron
photographed during the Battle of Britain.

Above: Spitfires of Nos. 222 and 603
Squadrons at Hornchurch at the time of the
Battle of Britain. Note the steam roller in
the background, to roll flat the filled-in bomb
craters on the airfield.
Right: The Messerschmitt 109E was the most
formidable opponent facing RAF Fighter
Command during the Battle of Britain.

fuel forced the Spitfires and Hurricanes
to return to their airfields, and then the
situation resolved itself. In fact, there
had never been any German aircraft in
the area. The fiasco cost the RAF three
aircraft destroyed; two Hurricanes shot
down by Spitfires of No. 74 Squadron
and a Blenheim shot down by anti-
aircraft fire. One RAF pilot was killed.

Following the action, Fighter Comm-
and launched a thoroughgoing official inquiry to determine what had
gone wrong and prevent a recurrence.
One lesson, which has to be re-learned
for each war, was the folly of opening

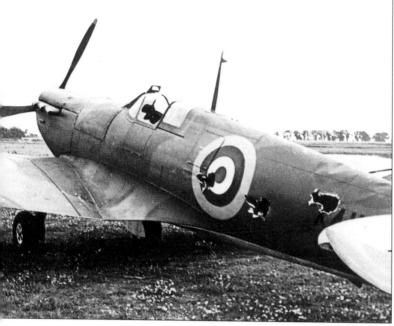

"During the Battle of Britain one had to take every opportunity to train new pilots. Young pilots would arrive on the squadron with only six or seven hours' flying time on the Spitfire. One or two practice sorties could make all the difference to their ability to survive in combat. When we were at 30 minutes available, I might ring operations and ask permission to take one of the new pilots into the air for 'follow my leader' practice. If one could take them up, one could point out their failings and tell them: 'You won't survive ten minutes in battle if you fly like that!' The object was to tell them why and lead them round, not to frighten them."

SQUADRON LEADER DONALD MACDONELL,
COMMANDER OF NO. 64 SQUADRON

Left: Spitfire X4110 had a service life of only 15 minutes. On the morning of 18 August 1940 this brand new aircraft arrived at No. 602 Squadron at Westhampnett as a replacement. Before there was time to paint on the squadron markings, Flight Lieutenant Dunlop Urie took it into action, and in an encounter with Me 109s the fighter suffered severe damage. Despite splinter wounds to both feet Urie landed the machine at base. The Spitfire's back was broken and it never flew again.

Spitfires and Hurricanes flew large numbers of sorties to cover the evacuation of Dunkirk

fire on aircraft that had not been positively identified as 'hostile'. Another was the danger of looking at the reports from one radar in isolation (other stations along the coast had reported seeing no aircraft approaching from the east, but the absence of plots had been ignored). A further lesson was the need to fit IFF (identification friend or foe) radar equipment in all RAF fighters, and the programme to build and install this equipment received top priority.

Spitfires encountered genuinely hostile aircraft for the first time on 16 October 1939, when aircraft of Nos. 602 and 603 Squadrons rose to intercept nine Junkers 88s running in to make a dive-bombing attack on Royal Navy warships in the Firth of Forth. Flight Lieutenant Pat Gifford of No. 603 Squadron shot down one of the bombers and Flight Lieutenant

nkerton and McKellar of No. 602 quadron destroyed another. A third 88 suffered damage.

The Spitfire first encountered German rcraft en masse on 21 May 1940, when ae rapid advance of the German army to Belgium and France brought the ar to within reach of Royal Air Force ghters operating from airfields in Kent. uring the weeks that followed, Spitfires nd Hurricanes flew large numbers of rties to cover the evacuation of Allied oops from Dunkirk.

■ BATTLE OF BRITAIN ■

t the beginning of July 1940, RAF ighter Command possessed 50 quadrons of modern single-seat fighters 31 with Hurricanes and 19 with pitfires. The Battle of Britain opened ith Luftwaffe attacks on convoys of hipping passing through the English

Above: Pilot Officer Robert Doe of No. 234 Squadron was credited with 11 enemy aircraft destroyed and two shared destroyed. He then moved to a Hurricane squadron and shot down three more. Doe suffered serious injuries during a crash landing in January 1941, and these prevented him flying for several months.
Above right: Dunlop Urie, his feet bandaged, waiting to be taken to hospital.
Right: Squadron Leader Donald MacDonell commanded No. 64 Squadron during the Battle, and was creadited with nine enemy aircraft destroyed and one shared destroyed. He was shot down in March 1941, and spent the rest of the war in captivity.

WAITING AT READINESS

During the Battle of Britain, RAF fighter squadrons waiting to go into action were held on the ground at what was known as Readiness 5 Minutes. The fighters sat in their earth-and-brick revetments around the perimeter of the airfield, and from time to time the ground crews would run the engines to warm the oil and ensure the planes could take off immediately. Squadron Leader Don MacDonell, commander of No. 64 Squadron during the Battle, explained what it was like having to wait on the ground until the next German attack was detected.

"When we were at Readiness the pilots would be relaxing at the dispersal area – reading, chatting, playing cards. Each Flight had a separate crew room, so no pilot was too far from his Spitfire. I would be out of my office, wearing flying kit and Mae West, with the Flight I was to lead on that day. Each pilot's parachute was laid out on the seat of his aircraft, with the straps laid over the armour plating at the back of the cockpit.

Every time the telephone rang there would be a ghastly silence. The orderly would answer it and often one would hear something like: 'Yes, Sir... yes, Sir... Yes, Sir... Sergeant Smith wanted on the phone.' And everyone would breathe again."

Channel. The purpose of the attacks was to disrupt the coastal traffic and also to force the Royal Air Force into action. As time passed, the fighting over the Channel became progressively more ferocious, and the Luftwaffe began sending free hunting patrols over southern England.

These actions were but a prelude to the main campaign by the Luftwaffe, which began on 13 August, aimed at destroying Fighter Command as an effective force. That day, German aircraft launched multi-pronged attacks on the Royal Navy bases at Portland and Southampton, and on the airfields at Detling and Eastchurch.

There were repeated attacks on Fighter Command airfields in the south of England

During the next three and a half weeks there were repeated attacks on Fighter Command airfields in the south of England. The Luftwaffe failed in its aim of knocking out Fighter Command, however. Every major airfield in the No. 11 Group area took hard knocks.

Above left: Flying Officer Leonard Haines of No. 19 Squadron was credited with eight enemy 'kills' and four shared destroyed. He died in a flying accident in April 1941.

Above: Squadron Leader Derek Boitel-Gill commanding No. 152 Squadron was credited with eight aircraft destroyed. He died in a flying accident in September 1941.

"SCRAMBLE!"

In Fighter Command the code-word 'Scramble' meant 'get airborne as rapidly as possible'. When pilots received the order, they ran as if their lives depended on it – because they did. Each 30-second delay in getting airborne meant 1,000ft (305m) less altitude they had when they met the enemy. And everyone knew that a Spitfire caught in the climb was easy meat for a Messerschmitt attacking in a dive. Squadron Leader Donald MacDonell explained the procedure for getting airborne:

"The orderly answering the telephone would shout "Scramble!" at the top of his voice and each pilot would dash for his aircraft. By the time one got there a mechanic would already have started the engine; the other would be holding the parachute up and help me strap it on. Once that was done I would clamber into the cockpit. He would pass my seat straps over my shoulders and help me fasten them. When I gave the thumbs-up he would slam shut the side door and I would pull tight the various straps. Next I would pull on my helmet, plug in the R/T lead and check that the engine was running properly. If all was well I would wave to the groundcrew to pull away the chocks, open the throttle, and move forward out of my blast pen and across the grass to the take-off position. Once there I would line up, open the throttle wide open and begin my take-off run with the rest of my pilots following as fast as they could. The whole thing, from the scramble order to the last aircraft leaving the ground, took about a minute and a half.

"As soon as Spitfires were all off the ground and climbing, I would inform operations. The Sector Controller would come back and tell me where he wanted me to go and at what altitude. While the squadron was forming up I would climb in a wide spiral at low boost, until everyone was in place. Then I would open up to a high throttle setting to get to altitude as fast as possible."

SPITFIRE FIGHTER DEPLOYMENT, SEPTEMBER 1940

Spitfire units on the afternoon of 14 September, before the decisive action of the Battle of Britain on the next day. The first figure indicates aircraft serviceable; figure in brackets shows aircraft unserviceable.

NO. 10 GROUP, HQ BOX, WILTSHIRE

Middle Wallop Sector
No. 152 Squadron 17 (2) Warmwell
No. 609 Squadron 15 (3) Middle Wallop
St Eval Sector
No. 234 Squadron 16 (1) St Eval
Group Total **48 (6)**

NO. 11 GROUP, HQ UXBRIDGE, MIDDLESEX

Biggin Hill Sector
No. 72 Squadron 10 (7) Biggin Hill
No. 92 Squadron 16 (1) Biggin Hill
No. 66 Squadron 14 (2) Gravesend

Hornchurch Sector
No. 603 Squadron 14 (5) Hornchurch
No. 41 Squadron 12 (6) Rochford
No. 222 Squadron 11 (3) Rochford
Tangmere Sector
No. 602 Squadron 15 (4) Westhampnett
Group Total **92 (28)**

NO. 12 GROUP, HQ WATNALL, NOTTING-HAMSHIRE

Duxford Sector
No. 19 Squadron 14 (0) Fowlmere
Coltishall Sector
No. 74 Squadron 14 (8) Coltishall
Wittering Sector
No. 266 Squadron 14 (5) Wittering
Digby Sector
No. 611 Squadron 17 (1) Digby
Kirton-in-Lindsey Sector
No. 616 Squadron 14 (4) Kirton-in-Lindsey
No. 64 Squadron 7 (3) Leconfield
 6 (3) Ringway
Group Total **86 (24)**

NO. 13 GROUP, HQ NEWCASTLE, NORTHUMBERLAND

Catterick Sector
No. 54 Squadron 15 (2) Catterick
Usworth Sector
No. 610 Squadron 14 (5) Acklington
Turnhouse Sector
No. 65 Squadron 15 (5) Turnhouse
Group Total **44 (12)**

Spitfires at Operational Training Units
 26 (24)

Spitfire production during week prior to 14 September 38

Replacement Spitfires held at Maintenance Units, 14 September 1940
Ready for immediate issue to units 47
Ready for issue within four days 10

Below left: Sergeant Basil Whall flew with No. 602 Squadron and was credited with seven enemy aircraft destroyed and two shared destroyed. In October 1940, he suffered fatal injuries when he tried to land his damaged aircraft after a combat sortie. **Below right:** Lieutenant Arthur 'Admiral' Blake, a Fleet Air Arm pilot loaned to RAF Fighter Command, flew with No. 19 Squadron. Credited with four enemy aircraft destroyed and one shared destroyed, he was shot down and killed in October 1940.

Above: The wrecked shell of the Supermarine factory at Woolston, pictured after the devastating German air attack on 26 September 1940.

However, there was an efficient damage-repair organization, and in the event only one airfield, that at Manston in Kent, was put out of action for more than a few hours. Only in rare instances were the raiders able to catch RAF fighters on the ground. By the time the German bombers arrived to deliver their attack on an airfield, the Spitfires and Hurricanes based there were usually airborne and well clear. Fighters able to fly but not fight took off on 'survival scrambles' with orders to keep clear of the area until the threat ha passed. Aircraft unable to fly we wheeled into the protective reve ments, or dispersed around the airfie where they were difficult to hit. As result of these measures, the front-li fighter units lost fewer than 20 fighte destroyed on the ground, despite th almost daily attacks on airfiel throughout a 25-day period.

On 7 September, the Luftwaf shifted its attack to London, concei trating its main effort against th sprawling dock area to the east the city. During the following wee there were three further attacks on th capital. Then on 15 September, Batt of Britain Day, the Luftwaffe mounte two separate raids on London.

"IT DEMONSTRATED THE DETERMINATION AND BRAVERY WITH WHICH THE TOMMIES WERE FIGHTING OVER THEIR OWN COUNTRY"

Early on the afternoon of 15 September 1940, as the Heinkel 111s of Bomber Geschwader 26 were passing Maidstone on their way home, the formation suddenly came under attack from Spitfires. Leutnant Roderich Cescotti, one of the German pilots, recalled:

"A few Tommies succeeded in penetrating our fighter escort. I saw a Spitfire dive steeply through our escort, level out and close rapidly on our formation. It opened fire, from ahead and to the right, and its tracers streaked towards us. At that moment a Bf 109, which we had not seen before, appeared behind the Spitfire and we saw its rounds striking the Spitfire's tail. But the Tommy continued his attack, coming straight for us, and his rounds slashed into our aircraft. We could not return the fire for fear of hitting the Messerschmitt. I put my left arm across my face to protect it from the plexiglass splinters flying around the cockpit, holding the controls with my right hand. With only the thin plexiglass between us, we were eye-to-eye with the enemy's eight machine-guns. At the last moment the Spitfire pulled up and passed very close over the top of us. Then it rolled on its back, as though out of control, and

went down steeply trailing black smoke. Waggling its wings, the Messerschmitt swept past us and curved in for another attack. The action lasted only a few seconds, but it demonstrated the determination and bravery with which the Tommies were fighting over their own country."

Cescotti's Heinkel had taken several hits, but he was able to hold position in formation. He made a normal landing at his base at Wevelghem in Belgium.

Almost certainly the courageous Spitfire pilot was Flying Officer Peter Pease of No. 603 Squadron, who was shot down at the time, the place, and in the manner described by Cescotti. When the blazing fighter smashed into the ground a few miles south-east of Maidstone, Pease was still in the cockpit.

The son of Sir Richard Pease, Arthur Peter Pease, studied at Eton and Cambridge University before joining the Royal Air Force at the beginning of the war. In July 1940, he was posted to No. 603 Squadron based at Dyce airfield near Aberdeen, and later that month he shared in the destruction of a Heinkel 111. Early in August the Squadron moved to

Hornchurch, north-east of London, to take part in the defence of southern England. On 3 September, Pease was credited with shooting down a Messerschmitt 109, and four days later his Spitfire suffered battle damage and he made a crash landing at Hornchurch. Just over a week later, on 15 September, Peter Pease died in action.

Above: Flying Officer Peter Pease of No. 603 Squadron, whose courageous attack is described by Roderich Cescotti.

"I FELT JOLLY GLAD TO BE DOWN ON THE GROUND WITHOUT HAVING CAUGHT FIRE"

"We were just going in to attack when somebody yelled 'Messerschmitts' over the R.T. and the whole squadron split up. Actually it was a false alarm. Anyway, being on my own I debated what to do. The bombers were my object, so I snooped in under the 110s and attacked the bombers (about 40–50 Heinkel 111s) from the starboard beam.

"I got in a burst of about three seconds when – Crash! and the whole world seemed to be tumbling in on me. I pushed the stick forward hard, went into a vertical dive and held it until I was below cloud. I had a look round. The chief trouble was that petrol was gushing into the cockpit at the rate of gallons all over my feet, and there was a sort of lake of petrol in the bottom of the cockpit. My knee and leg were tingling all over as if I had pushed them into a bed of nettles. There was a bullet hole in my windscreen where a bullet had come in and entered the dashboard, knocking away the starter button. Another bullet, I think an explosive one, had knocked away one of my petrol taps in front of the joystick, spattering my leg with little splinters and sending a chunk of something through the backside of my petrol tank near the bottom. I had obviously run into some pretty good crossfire from the Heinkels. I made for home at top speed to get there before all my petrol ran out. I was about 15 miles from the aerodrome and it was a heart-rending business with all that petrol gushing over my legs and the constant danger of fire. About five miles from the 'drome smoke began to come from under my dashboard. I thought the whole thing might blow up at any minute, so I switched off my engine. The smoke stopped. I glided towards the 'drome and tried putting my wheels down. One came down and the other remained stuck up. I tried to get the one that was down up again. It was stuck down. There was nothing for it but to make a one-wheel landing. I switched on my engine again to make the aerodrome. It took me some way and then began to smoke again, so I hastily switched off. I was now near enough and made a normal approach and held off. I made a good landing, touching down lightly. The unsupported wing slowly began to drop. I was able to hold it up for some time and then down came the wingtip on the ground. I began to slew round and counteracted as much as possible with the brake on the wheel which was down. I ended up going sideways on one wheel, a tail wheel and a wingtip. Luckily, the good tyre held out and the only damage to the aeroplane, apart from that done by the bullets, was a wingtip that is easily replaceable.

"I hopped out and went off to the M.O. to get a lot of metal splinters picked out of my leg and wrist. I felt jolly glad to be down on the ground without having caught fire."

PILOT OFFICER ERIC MARRS OF NO. 152 SQUADRON, DESCRIBING HIS ACTION ON 30 SEPTEMBER 1940

Left: **A pilot of No. 313 (Czech) Squadron running to his Spitfire during a scramble take-off.**

No. 11 Group of Fighter Command, which bore the brunt of the defence of the capital, possessed 310 serviceable single-seat fighters. Of that total, 218 were Hurricanes and 92 were Spitfires. To meet the two attacks on London, the RAF fighter controllers used the same defensive tactics against each. About one-third of the available squadrons, Hurricanes and Spitfires, engaged the raiding forces as they made their way across Kent to the capital. The purpose of these attacks was twofold: first, to destroy as many German bombers as possible; and secondly, to force the escorting Me 109s to fly at full throttle to ward off the British fighters and so deplete their limited supply of fuel. Meanwhile, the main body of defending fighters assembled over the east and south-east outskirts of London. It was there that the two great clashes occurred, and most of the aircraft were shot down.

■ BATTLE OF BRITAIN DAY ■

The first attack took place shortly before noon. The raiding force comprised 21 Messerschmitt 109 fighter-bombers and 27 Dornier 17 bombers, with an escort of about 180 Me 109s. The fighter-bombers were to attack rail targets throughout the London area, while the Dorniers were to hit the concentration of rail lines and junctions at Battersea. Two hours later, there was a much heavier attack on a series of targets in the London dock area, involving 114 Dornier 17s and Heinkel 111s escorted by some 450 Me 109s and a few Me 110s.

Above: WAAF mechanics helping the pilot strap into a Spitfire Mark II of No. 411 (Canadian) Squadron, at Digby in Lincolnshire in 1941.

Right: A few Mark II Spitfires were modified for the Air Sea Rescue role, and carried two cylindrical drums in parachutes in the rear fuselage. These contained an inflatable rubber dinghy and ration packs to drop to survivors.

During the late afternoon of the 15th, the Luftwaffe also launched smaller attacks on targets on the south coast. Twenty-six Heinkels bombed the Royal Navy base at Portland, and a small force of Messerschmitt 109 and 110 fighter-bombers tried unsuccessfully to hit the Supermarine plant at Southampton.

That day, 55 German aircraft were destroyed, most of them falling to fighter attack. The RAF lost eight Spitfires and 21 Hurricanes. The Spitfire force suffered a loss rate of 4.2 per hundred sorties, while the Hurricane force suffered a loss rate of 6.4 per hundred sorties. In action, the Spitfire's superior performance meant it had a 50 per cent better chance of survival compared with the Hurricane.

The German losses on 15 September fell far short of the 185 aircraft the defenders claimed as destroyed. Yet the action is rightly deemed to mark the climax of the Battle. Two days later, Adolf Hitler ordered an indefinite postponement of Operation Sealion, the planned invasion of Britain. The ships and barges concentrated at ports along the Channel coast returned to their normal tasks, and it was clear that the threat of invasion had passed.

■ MARK II ■

Towards the end of the Battle of Britain, the Spitfire Mark II entered service. Similar in most respects to the Mark I, the new variant was powered by the Merlin 12 engine, giving an additional 110 horsepower. With the installation of armour protection and additional items of equipment, however, the Mark II weighed 350lb (159kg) more than the early production Mark I. Because of this, the additional engine power merely restored the fighter's performance to its earlier level. The Spitfire emerged from the Battle of Britain with a proven record of success in the limited role of home-defence fighter. Yet this very success would inhibit its ability to achieve more in that role. Having suffered heavy losses during the Battle, the Luftwaffe gave up the idea of trying to mount large-scale daylight attacks on targets in Britain. If the Spitfire was to continue to play a major part in the war, it would have to do so in roles other than that of home-defence fighter. As we shall observe next, it had already started to do so.

MAINTAINING SPITFIRE PRODUCTION

On 26 September 1940, a raiding force of 59 Heinkel 111s mounted a devastating attack on the two main Supermarine factories at Woolston and Itchen. The bombers wrecked most of the factory buildings at both sites, striking a body blow at Spitfire production.

On the day following the attack, Lord Beaverbrook, Winston Churchill's tireless Minister of Aircraft Production, visited Southampton to inspect the damage. On his decision, the two wrecked factories were abandoned. Production of Spitfires was to be dispersed into several smaller units in towns and cities. Fortuitously, most of the machine tools and production jigs at Woolston and Itchen had survived the attack. Also, the final assembly hangers at Eastleigh airfield had not been touched. Supermarine executives toured Southampton, Winchester, Salisbury, Trowbridge, Reading and Newbury and the surrounding areas, looking at every large open building. Motor repair garages, laundries and bus stations were the obvious choices. Accompanying each Supermarine executive was a policeman who carried a letter of introduction from the Chief Constable of the area, requesting cooperation but giving no reason for the visit. Where a building was considered suitable for use in the dispersed production scheme, the not-always-delighted owner received official papers requisitioning the building. As each new site was acquired, the Spitfire production jigs and tools were brought in and set up.

By the end of October, 35 separate premises had been taken over for the programme and production had begun at 16 of them. Also by this time, the large-scale production had started at the huge purpose-built Nuffield organization factory at Castle Bromwich near Birmingham.

Never again would Spitfire production be as vulnerable to air attack as it had been in September 1940.

Above right and below: Following the attack on the Supermarine factories, Spitfire production was dispersed into several small units in the surrounding towns and cities. These photographs show Spitfire wing leading edges being manufactured at the requisitioned garage of Anna Valley Motors Ltd at Salisbury.

Below right: A remarkable photograph taken from a Messerschmitt 110 reconnaissance aircraft over Snodland, Kent, showing Spitfires of No. 64 Squadron climbing into position to intercept the aircraft. The Messerschmitt suffered severe damage in the ensuing engagement, and the radio operator was killed.

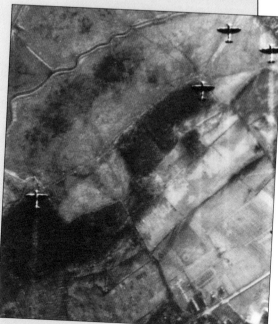

SPITFIRE SPYPLANES

In time of war, it is difficult to exaggerate the importance of aerial reconnaissance. To plan effective air attacks, staff officers require the best possible information on each target. They need to know where bombs should be aimed to cause maximum damage. They also need to know the layout of the defences around each target, so they can route the bombers to avoid the worst of them. Without such information, attacking forces will inflict less damage and suffer heavier losses than would otherwise be the case. The best source of such information is aerial photography.

Today, the idea of using an unarmed reconnaissance aircraft to make a high speed dash through enemy territory to photograph targets is well accepted. It was not always so. Before the Second World War, most air forces employed modified bombers to fly long-range reconnaissance missions. Lacking the performance to avoid the defences, these machines had to carry guns and gunners to fight their way through to targets.

Shortly before the outbreak of war, Flying Officer Maurice 'Shorty' Long-bottom, an enterprising young RAF officer, suggested a better means of securing reconnaissance photographs. In a memorandum, he set down his views on the future of strategic aerial recon-naissance. Longbottom suggested that reconnaissance should be done "in such a manner as to avoid the enemy fighters and AA defences as completely as pos-ible". The best way of doing that, he thought, was by "the use of a single small machine, relying solely on its speed, climb and ceiling to avoid detection. . ."

Longbottom believed the ideal aircraft would be a Spitfire with the guns, ammunition, radio and other unneces-sary equipment removed. With addi-tional fuel tanks and cameras installed in their place, he argued that such an aircraft would have the range to reach distant targets. It would, moreover, have the speed and altitude performance to penetrate the enemy defences at will.

The Air Ministry greeted Longbottom's memorandum with polite interest, but initially the paper was pigeon-holed. The RAF was desperately short of modern

Left: Compare the 1939 inset photograph with the main one, of Bullingen, taken in April 1944 from a Spitfire at the same altitude, with a camera fitted with a 36in (91.4cm) lens. Considerably more ground detail is visible. Comparison of these photos shows the great advances made in aerial cameras during the war years.

Top: Spitfire PR IC used for high-altitude photographic missions. This aircraft carried its vertically mounted cameras in a blister under the starboard wing, seen in the open position for the removal of the film magazines. *Middle:* Spitfire PR IF. This aircraft carried its vertically mounted cameras in the rear fuselage, and was fitted with blister fuel tanks under the wings to give it increased range.

Above: Spitfire PR IG used for low-altitude 'dicing' missions, to photograph targets beneath cloud. These aircraft wore a very pale shade of pink (the colour was the same as the bottom of cloud on overcast days). The window for the oblique camera is at the top left of the fuselage roundel.

RECONNAISSANCE VARIANTS

PR IA Original PR variant, one 5in (12.7cm) lens camera mounted in each wing. No additional fuel.

PR IB One 8in (20.3cm) lens camera in each wing. Additional fuel: 29 gallon (132 litre) tank in the rear fuselage.

PR IC As PR IB, but with the two 8in (20.3cm) lens cameras mounted in tandem in a blister fairing under the starboard wing. Additional fuel: 29 gallon (132 litre) tank in the rear fuselage; 30 gallon (136.5 litre) blister tank under the port wing.

PR ID First major redesign of the Spitfire for the reconnaissance role. Carried two 8in (20.3cm) or two 20in (50.8cm) lens cameras in the rear fuselage. Additional fuel: large fuel tank built integrally with the leading edge of the wing, capacity 114 gallons (518 litres); 29 gallon (132 litre) tank in the rear fuselage. This variant replaced the Marks IA, IB, IC and IF in front-line service during 1941. When fitted with the Merlin 45 engine it became the PR 5D, then it was redesignated as the PR Mark 4.

PR IE Designed for the low-altitude reconnaissance role; only one example produced. Oblique camera under each wing, pointing at right angles to the line

of flight. Additional fuel: 29 gallon (132 litre) tank in rear fuselage.

PR IF Carried two 8in (20.3cm) or two 20in (50.8cm) lens cameras in the rear fuselage. Additional fuel: 30 gallon (136.5 litre) blister tank under each wing; 29 gallon (132 litre) tank in the rear fuselage.

PR IG Designed for low-altitude reconnaissance role. One oblique camera mounted in the rear fuselage could point either to port or to starboard. In addition,

Above: A reconnaissance Spitfire at high altitude. When over enemy territory, pilots went to great pains to avoid leaving condensation trails, since these betrayed their position and made them vulnerable to fighter interception.

there was one 14in (35.6cm) and one 5in (12.7cm) lens camera mounted vertically in the rear fuselage. Additional fuel: 29 gallon (132 litre) tank in the rear fuselage.

Left and opposite right: Exterior and interior of the huge Spitfire production facility at Castle Bromwich, Birmingham. Morris Motors Ltd built the factory, under contract to the British Government. The plant produced some 12,000 Spitfires – more than half of the total. At its peak, it turned out 320 Spitfires per month.

Left: Dramatic low-altitude photograph of the German cruiser *Hipper* in dry dock, at the heavily defended port of Brest.

fighters, and needed every available Spitfire for the defence of Great Britain, Air Chief Marshal Dowding was unwilling to release these precious air-craft for other roles, no matter how persuasive the arguments might appear.

It took only six weeks of war to change people's minds. The main RAF

SPYPLANE PILOT

"During the early [photographic reconnaissance] missions there was no such thing as cockpit heating in our Spitfires. For the high altitude missions we wore thick suits with electrical heating. Trussed up in our Mae West and parachute, one could scarcely move in the narrow cockpit of the Spitfire. When flying over enemy territory one had to be searching the sky the whole time for enemy fighters. On more than one occasion I started violent evasive action to shake off a suspected enemy fighter, only to discover that it was a small speck of dirt on the inside of my perspex canopy!

"A big worry over enemy territory was that one might start leaving a condensation trail without knowing it, thus pointing out one's position to the enemy. To avoid that we had small mirrors fitted in the blisters on each side of the canopy, so that one could see the trail as soon as it started to form. When that happened one could either climb or descend until the trail ceased. If possible, we liked to climb above the trail's layer because then fighters trying to intercept us had first to climb through the trail's layer themselves and could be seen in good time."

PILOT OFFICER GORDON GREEN, SPITFIRE PILOT, PHOTOGRAPHIC RECONNAISSANCE UNIT

reconnaissance aircraft then in use, the low performance Blenheim, was quite inadequate for the task. Only rarely could they photograph targets any distance inside enemy territory, and they suffered heavy losses whenever they tried.

■ SECRET NEW UNIT ■

Following strong representations from the Air Ministry, Air Chief Marshal Dowding reluctantly agreed to release a couple of Spitfires for the reconnaissance role. The aircraft went to a highly secret new unit based at Heston north of London, headed by Wing Commander Sidney Cotton. Appropriately, one of the officers who helped him set up the unit was 'Shorty' Longbottom himself.

Cotton's first step was to modify the Spitfires for the new role and commence operations over enemy territory, to prove the validity of Longbottom's proposals. Each aircraft was fitted with a pair of cameras, mounted in each wing in the space previously occupied by the guns and ammunition boxes. Metal plates sealed off the empty gun ports, and groundcrewmen applied plaster of Paris to fill the joints in the skinning. Then each aircraft received a coat of polish to give it a smooth, high-gloss, finish. With these changes, the maximum speed of the reconnaissance Spitfires was about 12mph (about 20km/hr) faster than the fighter version.

In November 1939, the Spitfire reconnaissance unit under the cover-designation 'No. 2 Camouflage Unit' moved to Seclin near Lille in France to begin operational trials. On the 18th, Longbottom, now a Flight Lieutenant, took off to photograph the German city of Aachen and the nearby fortifications. Flying at 33,000ft (10,000m), a very high altitude in those days, he found navigation more difficult than expected. When his films were developed, they showed a strip of Belgian territory to the south of Aachen. Longbottom learned the lesson well, and when he returned to the area four days later, he made a successful photographic run over the German border defences.

During the weeks that followed, the two Spitfires photographed several targets in western Germany, including the Ruhr industrial area. Significantly, and in distinct contrast to the Blenheims, the Spitfires flew their missions without loss or even serious interference from the German defences.

Photographs taken from 33,000ft (10,000m) with 5in (12.7cm) focal-length cameras produced very small-scale pictures, however. The interpreters could pick out roads, railways, villages and major fortifications. But even with prints enlarged as much as the grain of the film allowed, it was not possible to see troop positions or individual vehicles. If the Spitfire's capabilities were to be fully exploited, longer-lens cameras would be needed. Work began to develop these. Apart from that proviso, the flights proved the essential soundness of Longbottom's proposals. As a result, Air Chief Marshal Dowding agreed to release a dozen more Spitfires for the reconnaissance role.

In January 1940, an improved photographic reconnaissance Spitfire was ready for operations, the PR IB (for details of this and other reconnaissance variants, see opposite; the earlier variant became known as the PR IA). In February, Longbottom demonstrated

the usefulness of the PR IB's additional range capability when he photographed the important German naval bases at Wilhelmshaven and Emden.

Soon afterwards, Cotton's unit was renamed the Photographic Development Unit, the new title revealing its true role for the first time. Early in 1940, the operations in France were reorganized and a further unit, No. 212 Squadron, formed at Seclin to conduct the Spitfire reconnaissance missions from there.

Below: A showpiece of the British aircraft industry, the Castle Bromwich plant had a constant stream of important visitors. Here, Winston Churchill is seen chatting with Alex Henshaw, Chief Test Pilot at the factory. Between the summer of 1940 and 1946, Henshaw personally tested no fewer than 2,360 Spitfires, about one in ten of those built.

■ LONG-RANGE VISION ■

In March 1940, a so-called 'long-range' reconnaissance version of the Spitfire appeared, the PR IC, with a further fuel tank to increase its reach. On 7 April, Longbottom took this aircraft to Kiel, the first RAF aircraft to photograph the important naval base since the outbreak of war.

Little over a month later, on 10 May 1940, German forces launched their powerful Blitzkrieg attack on France, Holland and Belgium. During the hectic weeks that followed, No. 212 Squadron photographed each stage of the relentless advance of the German Panzer columns. The squadron then withdrew to England, where its aircraft and personnel were incorporated in the PDU at Heston.

Thus far, the reconnaissance Spitfires had flown their missions at medium or high altitude, and photographed their targets from directly above. Most of the RAF's aerial photography would continue to be done that way, but there was another technique that allowed close-up shots or photography of targets below cloud. A few Spitfires were fitted with the so-called oblique camera installation, with a camera pointing

at right angles to the line of flight and few degrees below the horizontal. On July 1940, Flying Officer Alistair Taylo proved the value of the new installatior Despite a 700ft (213m) cloud base an heavy rain, which would have preclude vertical photography, he took good pho tographs of shipping inside Boulogn harbour as he flew past the outer mol From then on, low-altitude photography nicknamed 'dicing' because of the risk involved, became an important additior al role for the reconnaissance Spitfires.

Also in July 1940, the Photographi Development Unit underwent ye another name change. It became th Photographic Reconnaissance Uni (PRU), and at the same time Win Commander Geoffrey Tuttle replace Sidney Cotton as its commander. Th changes of name and commande made no difference to the way the uni operated, however.

> *Longbottom took the PR IC to Kiel, the first RAF aircraft to photograph the important naval base*

At the end of July, a further Spitfi reconnaissance variant appeared, th 'super-long-range' PR IF. This variar had a radius of action about 100 mil (160km) greater than the Type IC Operating from airfields in Eas Anglia, it could photograph targets a far afield as Berlin.

Throughout the summer of 1940 reconnaissance Spitfires kept a dai watch on the German preparations fo the invasion of Britain. Each day the sallied forth to photograph each of th ports along the Channel coast, observin the growing assemblies of barges an shipping at each. Then on 20 Septembe

"IT WAS ALL RATHER LIKE A FOX HUNT. . . "

'During the early [photographic reconnaissance] missions to cover Brest [in 1941] we lost about five pilots fairly quickly. After the first couple had failed to return the Flight Commander, Flight Lieutenant Keith Arnold, asked Benson [the headquarters of the reconnaissance units] to send some reserve pilots. They duly arrived. Both took off for Brest that evening and neither came back. That was a very sobering incident.

'The important thing with any photographic mission was to take the photos if one could, and get them back to base. As the 'boss' of PRU, Wing Commander Geoffrey Tuttle, often used to say, 'I want you to get home safely not just because I like your faces, but because if you don't the whole sortie will be a waste of time!' So it was no use trying to play hide and seek with the Luftwaffe. If one had lost surprise during the approach to a heavily defended target, the best thing was to abandon the mission. One could go back another time when things might be better. Looking back at my time with the PRU, I get a lot of satisfaction from the knowledge that although I played my part in the war, I never had to fire a shot in anger. In one sense we in the reconnaissance business had things easy. All the time it was impressed on us: bring back the photographs or, if you can't, bring back the aeroplane. An infantryman taking part in the Battle of Alamein could not suddenly decide 'This is ridiculous, I'm going home!' He just had to go on. But if we thought we had lost the element of surprise we were not only permitted to turn back, we were expected to do so. On the other hand there were times when I knew real fear. When one was 15 minutes out from Brest on a low altitude sortie, one's heart was beating away and as the target got nearer one's mouth got completely dry. Anyone who was not frightened at the thought of going in to photograph one of the most heavily defended targets in Europe, was not human.

"Whenever it was possible to photograph a target, flak could engage us: if we could see to photograph they could see to open up at us. But throughout my time as a reconnaissance pilot my luck held. I never once saw an enemy fighter, nor was my aircraft ever hit by flak. Indeed only once during the time we were flying those missions over Brest did one of our aircraft come back with any damage, and that was only minor. It was all rather like a fox hunt – either the fox got away unscathed or else it was caught and killed. There was rarely anything in between."

PILOT OFFICER GORDON GREEN, SPITFIRE PILOT, PHOTOGRAPHIC RECONNAISSANCE UNIT

---

ree days after Adolf Hitler's order to postpone the invasion, a reconnaissance pitfire returned bearing the first hard vidence of the change in German plans. s photographs of Cherbourg harbour owed that five destroyers and a rpedo boat had left the port since the revious reconnaissance. In the weeks at followed, almost every successive connaissance flight revealed fewer ships d barges in each port as the vessels sumed their normal tasks. The threat Great Britain had passed.

■ TO STETTIN ■

he 'long-range' and 'extra-long-range' rsions of the Spitfire opened new vistas r photographic reconnaissance and the rgets it could cover. Yet in terms of nge, the modified fighter could do even etter. Supermarine redesigned the wing take a huge additional fuel tank that ok up almost the entire leading edge ack to the main spar. In October 1940, e first Spitfires modified in this way, the R ID, became available for operations.

When carrying its full load of fuel, the R ID was difficult to handle, as Flight ieutenant Neil Wheeler explained. You could not fly it straight and level for the first half hour or hour after take-off. Until you had emptied the rear tank, the aircraft hunted the whole time. The centre of gravity was so far back that you couldn't control it. It was the sort of thing that would never have got in during peacetime, but war is another matter." Once part of the fuel load had been consumed, however, the Type D handled well, and its extra range gave it a dramatic extension of reconnaissance cover. On 29 October 1940, one of these aircraft photographed the port of Stettin on the Baltic (now Sczecin in Poland) and returned after 5 hours and 20 minutes airborne. Other remarkable missions followed in rapid succession: to Marseilles and Toulon in the extreme south of France, and to Trondheim in Norway.

The final reconnaissance variant of the Spitfire I was the Type G, optimized for the low-altitude photographic role with an oblique camera mounted in the rear fuselage. This version retained the fighter's standard armament of eight .303in (7.7mm) machine-guns to enable it to defend itself against enemy fighters.

By the beginning of 1941, the reconnaissance Spitfires possessed the range to photograph targets almost anywhere in western Europe. At this point in the Spitfire story, however, this account must return to the new challenges facing the fighter version, because, following developments in the war situation in northern Europe and the Mediterranean theatre, the aircraft was about to face a further severe test.

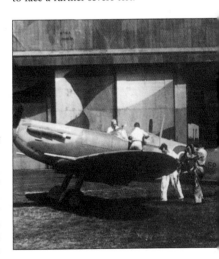

Above: Test pilots striding out to fly brand new Spitfires off the production line at Castle Bromwich. Alex Henshaw is second from the right.

n the spring of 1941, a new production version of the Spitfire appeared, the Mark V. This was fitted with the Merlin 45 engine which gave increases of, respectively, 140 and 330 horsepower over the versions fitted to the Marks I and II. The main production version of the Spitfire V carried an armament of two 20mm cannon and four .303in (7.7mm) machine-guns.

SPITFIRE V

Type Single-seat general-purpose fighter
Armament Four Hispano 20mm cannon with 120 rounds per gun, or two Hispano 2mm cannon with 120 rounds per gun and four Browning .303in (7.7mm) machine-guns with 350 rounds per gun, or eight .303in (7.7mm) Browning machine-guns with 350 rounds per gun; maximum bomb load two 250lb (113kg) bombs
Power plant One Rolls-Royce Merlin 45 liquid cooled V-12 engine developing 1,470hp
Dimensions Span 36ft 10in (10.98m), 32ft 6in (9.9m, clipped wings); length 29ft 11in (9.11m)
Weight Maximum loaded weight 6,070lb (2,752kg)
Performance Maximum speed 371mph at 20,000ft (597km/hr at 6,100m); service ceiling 38,000ft (11,585m)

Left and inset: Spitfire VC fitted with four 20mm cannon, being loaded on the aircraft carrier USS *Wasp* docked at Glasgow in April 1942. The wingtips had been removed and placed in the open cockpit, so that the aircraft could be brought by road from the nearby Abbotsinch airfield.
Above right: A remarkable modification to a Spitfire carried out in Germany, when the Daimler-Benz company at Stuttgart fitted a DB 605 engine into a captured Mark V and carried out flight tests with the combination.
Right: Spitfire in trouble – a still from a combat film taken by the Luftwaffe fighter ace Major Gerhard Schoepfel of Fighter Geschwader 26, showing cannon shells bursting on the fuselage.

Also during 1941, Fighter Command moved from the defensive to the offensive, mounting large-scale sweeps over occupied Europe. Simultaneously Spitfire production rose to a point where it exceeded losses, allowing an expansion in the number of units operating the fighter. During the Battle of Britain, 19 squadrons had operated Spitfires. By September 1941, there were 27. And by the end of 1941, Fighter Command had 46 squadrons equipped with Spitfires.

The Mark V had a performance significantly better than the earlier variants of the Spitfire, yet it was not good enough. In the summer of 1941, the Luftwaffe introduced a new and even more effective fighter into service: the Focke Wulf 190.

When this new German fighter first appeared in action over northern France, its performance came as a severe shock to Fighter Command. The Focke Wulf was 25–30mph (40–48km/hr) faster than the Spitfire V at most altitudes, and it could out-climb, out-dive and out-roll the British fighter. The Spitfire V's only advantage over its new opponent was that it could turn tighter.

Fortunately for the Royal Air Force, however, at this time the Luftwaffe was heavily committed to supporting the campaign in Russia. As a result, the size of the fighter force retained in the west, and in particular that part of it operating FW 190s, would remain relatively small.

■ SPITFIRES TO MALTA ■

The next major challenge to face the Spitfire came early in 1942, and this time the venue was far to the south. Malta was the cornerstone of Britain's strategy in the central Mediterranean. Torpedo-bombers operating from the island took

Left: In September 1942, the US manned 'Eagle' Squadrons of the RAF were officially transferred to the US Army Air Force with their aircraft. This aircraft went with No. 121 Squadron to become part of the 335th Fighter Squadron of the 4th Fighter Group.

Right: US Army Air Force mechanics carrying out an engine change on a Spitfire.

Below: Armourers of No. 72 Squadron cleaning the barrel and removing the ammunition drum from the Hispano 20mm cannon.

a steady toll of ships carrying supplies and reinforcements to sustain the Axis ground forces in North Africa. Yet the beleaguered island lay within 100 miles (160km) of Axis airfields in Sicily, and it suffered frequent and destructive air attacks. Malta's continued survival depended on the efficiency of her air defences, but the Hurricanes based on the island were outclassed by the Messerschmitt 109Fs opposing them.

Only the Spitfire V could engage the Me 109F on equal terms, but getting these aircraft to the island would be no easy task. The distance from Gibraltar to Malta was far beyond the Spitfire's

> ## When the new German fighter first appeared it came as a severe shock to Fighter Command

normal ferry range. Moreover, the strength of the Axis naval and air forces besieging the island precluded any large-scale delivery of fighters by sea. The Hurricanes already on Malta had been transported half way by aircraft carrier, which launched them to fly the rest of the way to the island. The Spitfires would have to use the same method, but even that would not be easy; from fly-off point to Malta was a distance of approximately 660 miles (1,062km).

To enable the Spitfire to reach Malta from a launch point, engineers at Supermarine designed a 90 gallon (409 litre) drop tank. The first delivery of Spitfires took place on 7 March 1942, when under

Operation Spotter 15 of them took off from HMS *Eagle*. Before the end of the month, the carrier made two further delivery runs, bringing to 31 the number of Spitfires flown to the island.

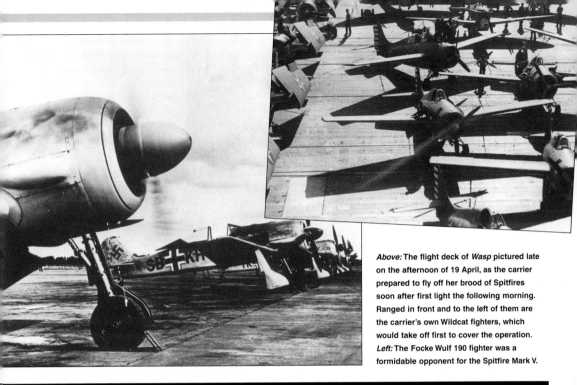

Above: The flight deck of *Wasp* pictured late on the afternoon of 19 April, as the carrier prepared to fly off her brood of Spitfires soon after first light the following morning. Ranged in front and to the left of them are the carrier's own Wildcat fighters, which would take off first to cover the operation.
Left: The Focke Wulf 190 fighter was a formidable opponent for the Spitfire Mark V.

SPITFIRE V VERSUS FOCKE WULF 190A

In July 1942, a Spitfire V was flown in a comparative trial against a captured Focke Wulf 190 fighter. During the past 10 months, RAF pilots had learned the hard way that they faced a formidable foe, but these trials revealed just how formidable that foe was. Excerpts from the official RAF report on the trials are given below.

Comparative speeds: The FW 190 was compared with a Spitfire VB from an operational squadron for speed and all-round manoeuvrability at heights up to 25,000ft (7,620m). The FW 190 is superior in speed at all heights, and the approximate differences are as follows:

At 2,000ft (610m) the FW 190 is 25–30mph (40–48km/hr) faster than the Spitfire 5B.

At 3,000ft (915m) the FW 190 is 30–35mph (48–56km/hr) faster than the Spitfire 5B.

At 5,000ft (1,525m) the FW 190 is 25mph (40km/hr) faster than the Spitfire VB.

At 9,000ft (2,744m) the FW 190 is 25–30mph (40–48km/hr) faster than the Spitfire 5B.

At 15,000ft (4573m) the FW 190 is 20mph (32km/hr) faster than the Spitfire 5B.

At 18,000ft (5,488m) the FW 190 is 20mph (32km/hr) faster than the Spitfire VB.

At 21,000 (6,400m) the FW 190 is 20–25mph (32–40km/hr) faster than the Spitfire VB.

Climb: The climb of the FW 190 is superior to that of the Spitfire VB at all heights. The best speeds for climbing are approximately the same, but the angle of the FW 190 is considerably steeper. Under maximum continuous climbing conditions, the climb of the FW 190 is about 450ft/min (137m/min) better up to 25,000ft (7,620m).

Dive: Comparative dives between the two aircraft have shown that the FW 190 can leave the Spitfire with ease, particularly during the initial stages.

Manoeuvrability: The manoeuvrability of the FW 190 is better than that of the Spitfire VB except in turning circles, when the Spitfire can quite easily out-turn it. The FW 190 has better acceleration under all conditions of flight and this must obviously be most useful during combat.

When the FW 190 was in a turn and was attacked by the Spitfire, the superior rate of roll enabled it to flick into a diving turn in the opposition direction. The pilot of the Spitfire found great difficulty in following this manoeuvre and even when prepared for it, was seldom able to allow the correct deflection. A dive from this manoeuvre enabled the FW 190 to draw away from the Spitfire which was then forced to break off the attack.

The above trials have shown that the Spitfire VB must cruise at high speed when in an area where enemy fighters can be expected. It will then, in addition to lessening the chances of being successfully 'bounced', have a better chance of catching the FW 190, particularly if it has the advantage of surprise.

Left: Following the launch of the Spitfires on deck, those in the hangar were brought up by lift and followed them into the air. This required slick timing, as this photograph shows. A Spitfire is about to begin its take-off; the aircraft ahead of it can be seen climbing away, just above the starboard wing. Meanwhile, the lift is already on the way to the hangar to pick up the next aircraft.

■ AMERICAN HELP ■

The Spitfires arrived in the nick of time. The Luftwaffe had stepped up it onslaught on the island and the defending fighter units were heavily outnumbered. With the air situation over Malta deteriorating rapidly, on 1 April Winston Churchill sent a personal telegram to President Roosevelt asking for help:

"Air attack on Malta is very heavy. There are now in Sicily about 400 German and 200 Italian fighters. Malta can only now muster 20 to 30 serviceable fighters. We keep feeding Malta with Spitfires in packets of 16 loosed from EAGLE carrier from about 600 miles west of Malta.

"This has worked a good many times quite well but EAGLE is now laid up for a month by defects in her steering gear . . . Therefore there will be a whole month without any Spitfire reinforcements. Would you be willing to allow your carrier WASP to do one of these trips provided details are satisfactorily agreed between the Navy Staffs? With her broad lifts, capacity and length, we estimate that WASP could take 50 or more Spitfires . . ."

Within three days of receiving the telegram, the US President agreed to the request. Six days after that, *Wasp* docked at Port Glasgow to load 47 Spitfires for the island. The mission was code-named Operation Calendar.

On 13 April, the American carrier set sail, and five days later she and her escorts passed through the Strait of Gibraltar. At first light on the 20th, off the coast of Algeria, the carrier began launching the Spitfires. Forty-six of the 47 fighters that took off reached Malta safely. Such was the ferocity of the air fighting, however, during the next few days most of the precious Spitfires had been destroyed in the air or on the

Above middle: Scene on the flight deck of USS *Wasp* on the morning of 9 May 1942, as the carrier prepares to launch her aircraft for the largest resupply of aircraft to Malta. In the background, also preparing to launch her Spitfires, is HMS *Eagle*.

Above: A soldier, a sailor and an airman carrying out refuelling and rearming of a Spitfire of No. 603 Squadron at Takali, Malta, in the spring of 1942. The blast pen was constructed from empty petrol tins filled with sand.

...ound. Again Malta was in crisis, and ...ain Mr Churchill asked the US ...esident to help. And again the latter ...ceded. The next resupply operation ...as to be the largest of them all, ...peration Bowery. The American ...rrier returned to Glasgow on 29 April ...d took on a further 47 Spitfires. By ...en HMS *Eagle* at Gibraltar had ...mpleted her repairs, and she took on ...further 17 fighters.

■ MALTA SAVED ■

...s *Wasp* entered the Mediterranean a ...cond time, *Eagle* set sail from ...ibraltar to join her. The two carriers ...d their escorts headed east together, ...d shortly after dawn on 9 May they ...unched their Spitfires. Sixty of the ...4 fighters that set out reached Malta. ...was sufficient to change the course ...f the battle. The island's air defences ...ere now strong enough to resist Axis ...r attacks, and could be topped up ...ith 'penny packets' of Spitfires deliv-...ed by the smaller Royal Navy carri-...rs. Never again would the island be in ...ich peril as it had been during the ...rst week in May 1942.

By the autumn of 1942, the RAF ...ossessed a more cost-effective method ...f delivering Spitfires from Malta

from Gibraltar. Supermarine engineers had modified the Mark V to fly the distance non-stop, by fitting a 170 gallon (772 litre) drop tank under the fuselage and a 29 gallon (132 litre) auxiliary tank in the rear fuselage. With a total fuel load of 284 gallons (1,290 litres), the modified Spitfire could fly the 1,100-mile (1,770km) distance in a single hop. That was as far as from London to St Petersburg in Russia, a remarkable feat for an aircraft designed originally as a short-range interceptor.

During October and November 1942, 17 Spitfires took off from Gibraltar to fly to Malta. All except one of them made it.

Had more Spitfires been required, they too would have flown to the island, but events in the North Africa theatre of operations had removed the need. The Allied victory at El Alamein, and the subsequent expulsion of Axis forces from Libya, lifted the siege of Malta.

Meanwhile, as we shall observe in the next chapter, engineers at Rolls-Royce had solved Fighter Command's most pressing problem. With a new variant of the Merlin engine the Spitfire would be able to engage the much-feared Focke Wulf 190 on equal terms.

BY SPITFIRE TO MALTA

Pilot Officer Michael Le Bas of No. 601 Squadron described his take-off in a Spitfire from the deck of USS *Wasp*. His heavily loaded aircraft carried a 90 gallon (409 litre) drop tank under the fuselage. Ahead lay a flight of 660 miles (1,062km), about as far as from London to Prague.

"The deck officer began rotating his checkered flag and I pushed forward the throttle to emergency override to get the last ounce of power out of my Merlin. The Spitfire picked up speed rapidly in its headlong charge down the deck, but not rapidly enough. The ship's bows got closer and closer and still I had insufficient airspeed and suddenly – I was off the end. With only 60 feet to play with before I hit the water, I retracted the undercarriage and eased forward on the stick to build up speed. Down and down went the Spitfire until, about 15 feet above the waves, it reached flying speed and I was able to level out. After what seemed an age but was in fact only a few seconds, my speed built up and I was able to climb away. Nobody had told me about that at the briefing! It had been a hairy introduction to flying off an aircraft carrier. Things had happened so quickly that there was no time to think. Perhaps it was just as well."

After the initial encounters with Focke Wulf 190s, Fighter Command made strong demands for an improved fighter with the performance to meet the new challenge. There could be no question of designing, building and bringing into service a completely new aircraft; on the most optimistic time scale, that would have taken at least four years. Fighter Command could not wait that long.

In fact, Rolls-Royce already had the answer to the problem in a new version of the Merlin. Previous versions of the engine used a single-stage supercharger.

The new engine employed a two-stage supercharger, in which the output from the first blower fed into the second to compress the charge of air further before it entered the carburettor. The two-stage supercharger gave a spectacular improvement in high-altitude performance. At 30,000ft (9,145m) the Merlin 45 engine with a single-stage supercharger developed about 720 horsepower. At the same altitude the same basic engine fitted with a two-stage supercharger developed about 1,020 horsepower, an increase of more than 40 per cent. The extra plumbing added only about 200lb (90kg) to the weight of the engine and increased its length by 9in (23cm). At the end of September 1941, three weeks after the debut of the Focke Wulf FW 190, an experimental Spitfire fitted with the Merlin incorporating the two-stage supercharger began flight testing.

There could be no question of designing, building and bringing into service a completely new aircraft

Opposite: A Spitfire VII, the high-altitude interceptor version of the famous fighter. Note the distinctive long-span wing with pointed tips, a recognition feature of this particular variant.

SPITFIRE MARK IX

Type Single-seat general-purpose fighter and fighter-bomber
Armament Two Hispano 20mm cannon with 120 rounds per gun, four Browning .303in (7.7mm) machine-guns with 350 rounds per gun; or two Hispano 20mm cannon with 120 rounds per gun and two Browning .5in (12.7mm) machine-guns with 250 rounds per gun; maximum bomb load one 50lb (226kg) bomb and two 250lb (113kg)

Power plant One Rolls-Royce Merlin 61, 63 or 70 liquid cooled V-12 engine with two-stage supercharger; Merlin 65 developed 1,565 hp
Dimensions Span 40ft 2in (12.85m, pointed wingtips), 36ft 10in (10.98m, normal wingtips) or 32ft 6in (9.9m, clipped wings); length 30ft 0in (9.14m)

Weight Maximum loaded weight 7,500lb (3,400kg)
Performance Maximum speed 40mph at 25,000ft (657km/hr at 7,622m); service ceiling 43,000ft (13,110m)

Below: Spitfire IX of No. 402 (Canadian) Squadron.

TURNING POINT IN AN AIR WAR

On the afternoon of 30 July 1942, Flight Lieutenant Donald Kingaby of No. 64 Squadron scored his 16th aerial victory. Afterwards he reported:

"I sighted approximately 12 FW 190s 2,000ft [610m] below us at 12,000ft [3,658m] just off Boulogne proceeding towards French coast. We dived down on them and I attacked a FW 190 from astern and below giving a very short burst, about half a second, from 300yd. I was forced to break away as I was crowded out by other Spits. I broke down and right and caught another FW as he commenced to dive away. At 14,000ft [4,268m] approx. I gave a burst of cannon and M/G, 400yd range hitting E/A along fuselage. Pieces fell off and E/A continued in straight dive nearly vertical. I followed E/A down to 5,000ft [1,525m] over Boulogne and saw him hit the deck just outside the town of Boulogne and explode and burn up. Returned to base at 0ft."

The combat report was little different from many others in the summer of 1942, yet this air combat marked a significant turning point in the air war over Europe. It was the first time the Spitfire Mark IX had encountered the Focke Wulf 190 in action. The latest variant of the British fighter showed that it could take on its once-feared opponent on equal terms. For the Luftwaffe, that action marked the beginning of the end of the easy-going superiority its fighters had enjoyed for most of the previous year. It would never regain that position.

Initially there were difficulties in getting the supercharger to work properly, but by the end of the year these had been resolved. The Merlin 61 Spitfire showed itself to be considerably faster than any previous version, with a maximum speed of 414mph at 27,200ft (667km/hr at 8,300m). Its rate of climb was also considerably better than that of the Spitfire V, and its service ceiling was over 41,000ft (12,500m).

■ THREE NEW VARIANTS ■

Fighter Command and Supermarine both knew a good thing when they saw it, and the new Merlin engine quickly spawned three more variants of the Spitfire. The Spitfire VII was a high-altitude interceptor version, with a pressurized cabin and a longer wingspan giving increased area. Its airframe was redesigned and strengthened to compensate for the increases in engine power and weight the fighter had incurred previously. The second of the new variants, the Spitfire VIII, was similar to the Mark VII but lacked the pressurized cabin of that type.

These two versions required a large amount of redesign, however, as well as retooling of the production lines. The changes would take time, and

neither version would be available in quantity until the spring of 1943.

In the meantime, Fighter Command needed a fighter to counter the FW 190, and it needed it quickly. The solution arrived in the form of the Spitfire IX, which was essentially a Mark V with the minimum of modification necessary to take the Merlin 61 engine. Measured against peacetime stressing factors, the airframe of the Mark V was not really strong enough to accept the additional engine power and the increases in all-up weight. In wartime, however, the RAF was prepared to accept this deficiency in the name of operational expediency. No fighter pilot was going to reject the Spitfire IX in favour of the Mark V for that reason alone!

Left and above: A damaged aircraft repaired and returned to service was as valuable as a new aircraft built, and the RAF salvage teams and repair organization played a valuable role. This Spitfire of No. 403 (Canadian) Squadron had crash-landed in a suspected minefield in Normandy. After a sweep of the area to ensure that it was safe to approach the aircraft, the fighter was dismantled and loaded on to a 'Queen Mary' transporter.

The first production Spitfire IXs arrived at No. 64 Squadron at Hornchurch during June 1942, and the unit resumed operations with the new variant at the end of July. The new Spitfire quickly demonstrated that it was the equal of the Focke Wulf 190 in combat. Proof of this came a few weeks later, when a German pilot inadvertently landed his FW 190 at Pembrey in South Wales. The RAF carried out detailed flight tests with the captured aircraft to determine its exact performance, and then had it fly

SPITFIRE IX VERSUS FOCKE WULF 190A

In July 1942, a Spitfire IX was flown in a comparative trial against a captured Focke Wulf 190. Considering they were quite different aircraft, the similarities in performances were remarkable. Excerpts from the official trials report are given below.

Comparative speeds: The FW 190 was compared with a fully operational Spitfire IX for speed and manoeuvrability at heights up to 25,000ft (7,620m). The Spitfire IX at most heights is slightly superior in speed to the FW 190, and the approximate differences in speeds at various heights are as follows:

At 2,000ft (610m) the FW 190 is 7–8mph (11–13km/hr) faster than the Spitfire IX.

At 5,000ft (1,524m) the FW 190 and the Spitfire IX are approximately the same.

At 8,000ft (2,44m) the Spitfire IX is 8mph (13km/hr) faster than the FW 190.

At 15,000ft (4,573m) the Spitfire IX is 5mph (8km/hr) faster than the FW 190.

At 18,000ft (5,488m) the FW 190 is 3mph (5km/hr) faster than the Spitfire IX.

At 21,000ft (6,400m) the FW 190 and the Spitfire IX are approximately the same.

At 25,000ft (7,622m) the Spitfire IX is 5–7mph 98–11km/hr) faster than the FW 190.

Climb: During comparative climbs at various heights up to 23,000ft (7,012m), with both aircraft flying under maximum continuous climbing conditions, little difference was found between the two aircraft, although on the whole the Spitfire IX was slightly better. Above 22,000ft (6,707m) the climb of the FW 190 is falling off rapidly, whereas the climb of the Spitfire IX is increasing.

Dive: The FW 190 is faster than the Spitfire IX in a dive, particularly during the initial stage. This superiority is not as marked as with the Spitfire VB.

Manoeuvrability: The FW 190 is more manoeuvrable than the Spitfire IX except in turning circles, when it is out-turned without difficulty. The superior rate of roll of the FW 190 enabled it to avoid the Spitfire IX if attacked when in a turn, by flicking over into a diving turn in the opposition direction. As with the Spitfire VB, the Spitfire IX had great difficulty in following this manoeuvre.

The Spitfire IX's worst heights for fighting the FW 190 were between 18,000 and 22,000ft (5,486m and 6,707m) and below 3,000ft (914m). At these heights, the FW 190 is a little faster.

The initial acceleration of the FW 190 is better than the Spitfire IX under all conditions of flight, except in level flight at such altitudes where the Spitfire has a speed advantage. Then, provided the Spitfire is cruising at high speed, there is little to choose between the acceleration of the two aircraft.

The general impression gained by the pilots taking part in the trials is that the Spitfire IX compares favourably with the FW 190. Provided the Spitfire has the initiative, it undoubtedly has a good chance of shooting down the FW 190.

MARK VII

Type Single-seat high-altitude interceptor fighter with pressurized cabin

Armament Two Hispano 20mm cannon with 120 rounds per gun, four Browning .303in (7.7mm) machine-guns with 350 rounds per gun; aircraft assigned to ultra high-altitude interception duties sometimes carried only the four .303in machine-guns

Power plant One Rolls-Royce Merlin 61, 64 or 71 liquid cooled V-12 engine with two-stage supercharger; Merlin 61 developed 1,565hp

Dimensions Span 40ft 2in (12.85m, pointed wingtips) or 36ft 10in (10.98m normal wingtips); length 30ft 0in (9.15m)

Weight Maximum loaded weight 8,000lb (3,628kg)

Performance (Rolls-Royce Merlin 71 engine) maximum speed 424mph at 29,500ft (682km/hr at 8,994m); service ceiling 45,100ft (13,750m)

mock combats with each of the main Allied fighters. The comparison with the Spitfire IX (see preceding page) revealed that the two fighters were uncannily similar in performance.

■ MARK IX IN SERVICE ■

Initially, the Mark IX units represented only a small proportion of the Spitfire force, but even so the new variant had an immediate impact on the air situation. In combat, it was impossible to distinguish it from the Mark V, and FW 190 pilots could never be certain which Spitfire variant they faced. As a result, the German fighters became markedly less aggressive and RAF fighter losses fell appreciably.

The first major action involving Spitfire IXs was on 19 August 1942, during the amphibious raid on Dieppe on the French coast. Four squadrons flew the new variant that day, and in the course of intensive air operations they mounted 14 squadron-sized missions comprising about 150 sorties. These resulted in claims of six enemy aircraft destroyed and two probably destroyed, for the loss of seven fighters. By the spring of 1943, the Spitfire IX equipped most of the RAF's single-seat fighter squadrons based in Great Britain. Perhaps surprisingly, the re-engineered variants of

the Spitfire intended to replace the Mark IX saw rather less use. The feared high-altitude attacks on Great Britain failed to materialize, and the order for Mark VIIs was greatly reduced. Production ended early in 1944, after about 140 had been built.

Below: Spitfire Mark VIIIs of No. 417 (Canadian) Squadron based at Canne, Italy, in 1944. These aircraft were fitted with pointed wingtips for high-altitude operations, as employed on the Mark II.

Left: The Spitfire Mark XVI was similar to the Mark IX, but was powered by the version of the Merlin engine built under licence by the American Packard Company. Late production Spitfire IXs and XVIs featured cut-down fuselages and bubble canopies, as seen on these Mark XVIs undergoing final assembly at Castle Bromwich in the spring of 1945.

Below left: Floatplane conversion of the Spitfire. A small number of aircraft were modified in this way, but none saw action.

BUBBLE CANOPY

In most cases where Spitfires were shot down by enemy fighters, the victim never saw his assailant in time to take effective evasive action. Most such attacks were mounted from the fighter's blind zone, below and behind. Any modification that reduced the likelihood of a surprise attack would increase the fighter's chances of survival in combat.

The answer was to cut back the rear fuselage behind the cockpit, and fit the fighter with a bubble canopy. A Spitfire modified in this way flew for the first time in the summer of 1943. The manufacturer's trials showed that the change brought no significant deterioration in the aircraft's handling characteristics. Experienced service pilots were hugely impressed with the improvement in view from the bubble canopy. Their report stated:

"This is an enormous improvement over the standard Spitfire rear view. The pilot can see quite easily round to his fin and past it, almost to the further edge of the tailplane, i.e. if he looks over his left shoulder he can practically see to the starboard tip of the tail. By banking the aircraft slightly during weaving action, the downward view to the rear is opened up well."

Production Spitfire Mark IXs, XIVs and XVIs fitted with bubble canopies began reaching the operational squadrons early in 1945 and they immediately became popular with pilots.

By the time the Mark VII became available in quantity, in the spring of 1943, the FW 190 menace over north-west Europe had been contained. The entire 1,658-aircraft production run of this variant went overseas to units operating in the Middle East, the Far East and Australia.

The 'stop-gap' version of the Merlin 61 Spitfire, the Mark IX, continued in production a lot longer than anyone had expected. Between them, the Supermarine and Castle Bromwich plants turned out nearly 6,000 of them.

The Spitfire XVI airframe was almost identical to that of the Mark IX, but it was powered by a version of the Merlin built by the American Packard Company. Late production Spitfire IXs and XVIs featured cut-down fuselages and bubble canopies – features which gave the pilot greatly improved vision behind and below the fighter.

The introduction of the Merlin 60 series improved the performance of the Spitfire to the point where it could fight the FW 190 on equal terms. Yet engineers at Rolls-Royce were not content to rest on their laurels. As we shall observe in the next chapter, they had something even better on offer.

ENTER THE GRIFFON

In 1939, Rolls-Royce had begun development of a larger engine than the Merlin, later named the Griffon. With a cubic capacity of 65 gallons (36.75 litres), the new engine was one-third larger than its predecessor. The initial production version, with a single-stage supercharger, developed 1,735 horsepower. By clever positioning of components, the designers kept the length of the Griffon to within 3in (7.5cm), and the weight to within 600lb (272kg) of the equivalent figures for the Merlin. Moreover, the new engine's frontal area was little greater than that of its predecessor.

The Spitfire was an obvious application for the new engine, and in November 1941 an experimental Griffon prototype, the Mark IV, began flight testing. The aircraft had a maximum speed of 372mph at 5,700ft (600km/hr at 1,740m), which increased to 397mph at 18,000ft (640km/hr at 5,500m).

SPITFIRE XII

Type Single-seat fighter optimized for operations at low and medium altitudes
Armament Two Hispano 20mm cannon with 120 rounds per gun, four Browning .303in (7.7mm) machine-guns with 350 rounds per gun
Power plant One Rolls-Royce Griffon 4 liquid cooled V-12 engine with single-stage supercharger developing 1,735 horsepower
Dimensions Span 32ft 7in (9.93m); length 30ft 9in (9.37m)

Weight Maximum loaded weight 7,400lb (3,356kg)
Performance Maximum speed 389mph at 12,500ft (626km/hr at 3,810m); service ceiling 37,350ft (11,387m)

Below: The first Griffon-powered Spitfire, pictured after the aircraft had been modified to become the prototype Mark XII low-altitude fighter.

To counter the threat, the RAF issued a requirement for a low-altitude interceptor

At about this time, the Luftwaffe commenced tip-and-run attacks on towns on the south and east coasts of England. Small forces of fighter-bombers ran in at low altitude to avoid radar detection, giving the defenders little time to react. To counter the threat, the RAF issued a requirement for a low-altitude interceptor. The Griffon Spitfire offered the best performance at low altitude, and this became the

Left: Mark XIV Spitfire of No. 402 (Canadian) Squadron. This version was the most effective variant to operate in the air superiority role during the Second World War.

SPITFIRE XIV

Type Single-seat fighter and fighter-reconnaissance aircraft
Armament Two Hispano 20mm cannon with 120 rounds per gun, four Browning .303in (7.7mm) machine-guns with 350 rounds per gun; or two Hispano 20mm cannon with 120 rounds per gun and two Browning .5in (12.7mm) machine-guns with 250 rounds per gun; fighter reconnaissance version carried an oblique-mounted camera in the rear fuselage

Power plant One Rolls-Royce Griffon 65 liquid cooled V-12 engine with two-stage supercharger developing 2,035hp
Dimensions Span 36ft 1in (10.98m normal wingtips) or 32ft 7in (9.93m, clipped wings); length 32ft 8in (9.96m)
Weight Maximum loaded weight 10,065lb (4,565kg)
Performance Maximum speed 439mph at 24,500ft (707km/hr); service ceiling 43,000ft (13,110m)

prototype for the Mark XII fighter. Supermarine received a production order to build 100 examples.

Like the Mark IX, the early production Mark XIIs used Mark V airframes with the minimum of modification necessary to take the new engine. Production Mark XIIs all had clipped wings, to give greater speed at low alti-

tude and greater rate of roll at all altitudes. Compared with the Mark IX, the Mark XII was 14mph (22km/hr) faster at sea level and 8mph faster at 10,000ft (13km/hr at 3,050m). But above 20,000ft (6,100m), performance fell away rapidly, and the Mark XII became progressively slower than the Mark IX.

In the spring of 1943, Nos. 41 and 91 Squadrons re-equipped with Mark XIIs and commenced operations from Hawkinge airfield near Folkestone. The units flew standing patrols against enemy fighter-bombers attacking coastal targets, and on 25 May No. 91 Squadron scrambled six fighters to engage FW 190 fighter-bombers attacking Folkestone. In the ensuing combat the Spitfires claimed the destruction of six raiders, without loss to themselves.

This action proved to be a rare success for the Mark XII, however. Although it was faster than the opposing fighter types at low and medium altitudes, this was of little value during offensive sweeps over France. German fighter pilots preferred to remain at altitude, coming down only to deliver high-speed diving attacks before making zoom climbs back to altitude. Rarely would they let themselves be drawn into turning fights with Spitfires below 20,000ft (6,096m).

An obvious next step for the Spitfire was to fit it with a Griffon with a two-stage supercharger. The new engine, the Griffon 65, appeared in the spring of 1943, and developed an impressive 1,540 horsepower for take-off and 2,035hp at 7,000ft (2,134m). Six Spitfire VIIIs were modified to take the new engine, and became prototypes for the Mark XIV.

Flight tests with pre-production Mark XIVs revealed it to be an extremely effective fighter, giving a huge improvement in performance over the Mark IX. During comparative trials against a captured FW 190 and a Messerschmitt 109G, the Spitfire XIV showed itself superior to the German fighters in almost every respect.

The new variant went into production in the autumn of 1943, and by the following spring Nos. 91, 322 and 610 Squadrons had received Mark XIVs. All three units were fully operational in June when the V.1 flying bomb attacks on London commenced.

■ SPITFIRE V FLYING BOMB ■

Although the V.1s flew a straight and predictable path, usually they were not easy targets. The majority flew at speeds around 350mph (563km/hr), although the fastest reached 420mph (675km/hr) and the slowest came in at around 230mph (370km/hr). There were similar variations in altitude. Most flying bombs crossed the coast at between 3,000 and 4,000ft (915 and 1,220m), but the highest came in at around 8,000ft (2,440m) and the lowest

flew at treetop height – which frequently led to their early demise!

Protecting the capital were four separate layers of defences. The first layer, extending from mid-Channel to about 10 miles (16km) short of the south coast, was the Outer Fighter Patrol Area where Spitfires and other fighters could engage the flying bombs. Next came the Gun Belt, with more than 2,500 AA guns of all calibres positioned along the strip of coast between Beachy Head and Dover; this was off-limits to fighters, allowing gunners freedom to shoot at anything that came within range. From 10 miles (16km) inland to 10 miles (16km) short of London was the Inner Fighter Patrol Area, where more fighters engaged the V.1s. The final layer, also off-limits to fighters, was the barrage

Although the V.1s flew a straight and predictable path, usually they were not easy targets

balloon zone. This began 10 miles (16km) short of the London built-up area and ended at its outskirts, and above it there hovered more than 1,000 of the ungainly gasbags.

All available squadrons with Mark XIVs redeployed to airfields in Kent to defend the capital. Of the V.1s shot down by fighters, the great majority fell out of control and exploded on striking the ground. A few detonated in mid-air, but there was little risk of serious damage to the fighter unless it was within 150yd (137m) of the explosion. Fighters often suffered minor damage, however, if they struck flying pieces from the missile, or if they flew through the cloud of burning petrol from the fuel tank. Another method of bringing down a V.1 was to fly alongside it, place the fighter's wing under that of the flying bomb and then bank steeply to flip the missile out of control.

■ AIR SUPERIORITY FIGHTER ■

At the end of August 1944, Allied ground forces advancing along the north coast

---

SPITFIRE XIV COMPARED WITH FOCKE WULF 190A

Early in 1944, the Air Fighting Development Unit at Duxford flew a Spitfire XIV in a comparative trial against a captured Focke Wulf 190A. Excerpts from the official trials report are given below:

Maximum speeds: From 0–5,000ft (0–1,525m) and 15,000–0,000ft (4,573–6,100m) the Spitfire XIV is only 20mph (32km/hr) faster; at all other heights it is up to 60mph (97km/hr) faster.

Maximum climb: The Spitfire XIV has a considerably greater rate of climb than the FW 190 A at all altitudes.

Dive: After the initial part of the dive, during which the FW 190 gains slightly, the Spitfire XIV has a slight advantage.

Turning circle: The Spitfire XIV can easily turn inside the FW 190. Though in the case of a right-hand turn, this difference is not quite so pronounced.

Rate of roll: The FW 190 is very much better.

Conclusions: In defence, the Spitfire XIV should use its remarkable maximum climb and turning circle against any enemy aircraft. In the attack it can afford to 'mix it' but should beware of the quick roll and dive. If this manoeuvre is used by an FW 190 and the Spitfire XIV follows, it will probably not be able to close the range until the FW 190 has pulled out of its dive.

SPITFIRE XIV COMPARED WITH Me 109G

Early in 1944, the Air Fighting Development Unit at Duxford flew a Spitfire XIV in a comparative trial against a captured Messerschmitt 109G, the latest sub-type of the famous German fighter. Excerpts from the official trials report are given below:

Maximum speed: The Spitfire XIV is 40mph (64km/hr) faster at all heights except near 16,000ft (4,878m), where it is only 10mph (16km/hr) faster.

Maximum climb: The same result – at 16,000ft (4,877m) the two aircraft are identical, otherwise the Spitfire XIV out-climbs the Me 109G. The zoom climb is practically identical when the climb is made without opening the throttle. Climbing at full throttle, the Spitfire XIV draws away from the Me 109G quite easily. **Dive:** During the initial part of the dive, the Me 109G pulls away slightly, but when a speed of 380mph (611km/hr) is reached, the Spitfire XIV begins to gain on the Me 109G.

Turning circle: The Spitfire XIV easily outturns the Me 109G in either direction. **Rate of roll:** The Spitfire XIV rolls much more quickly. **Conclusion:** The Spitfire XIV is superior to the Me 109G in every respect.

Below: During mock combats, the Me 109G was no match for the Spitfire XIV.

f France overran the last of the V.1 launching sites in the Pas de Calais. The ,617th and last flying bomb launched om that area crossed the south coast of ngland on the morning of 1 September.

Following the capture of the V.1 tes, the Spitfire XIV squadrons redeloyed to airfields in Belgium, to esume operations against conventionl enemy aircraft. Four further quadrons joined them soon afterards, Nos. 41, 130, 350 and 403 quadrons. For the remainder of the ar, the Mark XIV was the main air uperiority fighter operated by the

Royal Air Force in the skies over northern Europe.

The Mark XXI was intended as the 'definitive' fighter variant of the Spitfire, and had the war continued into 1946, it was set to become the RAF's main air superiority type. Powered by the Griffon 65 engine, it featured a completely redesigned wing with a much-strengthened internal structure. It carried the four 20mm cannon armament as standard. These changes added significant weight to aircraft, however, and early production machines had unpleasant handling characteristics. It took a few months to

iron out these bugs, and as a result the variant entered service only during the final few weeks of the war.

The delay in bringing the Mark XXI into action had no effect on the air war in Europe, for the Allied Air Forces defeated the Luftwaffe with the fighter types in service. Before we finish with the Second World War, however, it is necessary to review developments of the Spitfire for roles other than air combat. In the next chapter we shall observe the work done to improve the effectiveness of reconnaissance variants.

SPITFIRE FIGHTER-BOMBER

Winston Churchill once commented that "Air power is the most difficult of all forms of military force to measure, or even to express in precise terms." One can apply those same words to air superiority. Certainly, once the enemy air force is driven from the skies, the side with air superiority possesses a great advantage. However, to exploit this advantage, types of aircraft other than the pure fighter must be brought into play. Bombers, transports and reconnaissance aircraft can then capitalize on the situation and mount effective operations to support the land battle. To assist with this, part of the fighter force will relinquish air-to-air operations and join in the attack on ground targets.

By the time of the Normandy invasion, in June 1944, the Luftwaffe had been weakened to such a point that it was rarely able to operate over northern France. Having thus secured air superiority, many Spitfire units switched to the fighter-bomber role. These aircraft became the bane of the existence of German ground troops, as they bombed and strafed anything that moved in the rear areas. Such attacks made movement on the ground extremely hazardous during the daylight hours.

■ TARGET ROMMEL ■

An action by Spitfire fighter-bombers that had far-reaching consequences for the land battle occurred on 17 July 1944. That day, Field Marshal Erwin Rommel, commander of German ground forces in Normandy, needed to travel urgently to a sector of the front where an Allied breakthrough seemed

imminent. A flight of Mustangs on low-level reconnaissance observed the staff car speeding along a road near Lisieux, and reported their find. Spitfires of No. 602 Squadron, flying an armed reconnaissance over the area, were immediately ordered to investigate the sighting.

Squadron Leader Chris Le Roux, the formation leader, spotted the car and carried out a low-altitude strafing attack with cannon and machine-guns. He scored several hits and, its driver dead at the wheel, the car ran off the road and crashed into a tree.

Opposite: A pair of Spitfire IX fighter-bombers of No. 601 Squadron about to take off from Fano, Italy, to attack a target in enemy territory. The nearer aircraft carries a 500lb (226kg) bomb under the fuselage, and the aircraft in the background carries a 250lb (113kg) bomb.
Below and overleaf: Mark IXs fitted with two 250lb (113kg) bombs under the wings.

"THE EFFECT OF AIR SUPERIORITY"

"... we always knew when we were flying over the front line either when starting out on a reconnaissance mission or when returning: the contrast was astonishing, for in German occupied territory not a thing moved; perhaps a solitary vehicle would be observed, but as soon as the driver or look-out saw an aeroplane the vehicle stopped. Over our own territory masses of tents and convoys were to be seen; and that was the effect that air superiority, or the complete lack of it, had on land forces and their everyday existence."

GROUP CAPTAIN G. MILLINGTON, COMMANDER NO. 285 (RECONNAISSANCE) WING IN ITALY, 1944, IN HIS BOOK *THE UNSEEN EYE*

Rommel suffered a fractured skull and severe concussion, and had to be replaced at a critical stage in the land battle.

■ BOMB LOADS CARRIED ■

The bomb loads carried by Spitfires flying ground attack missions depended on the nature of the target and its distance from base. The greater the distance the aircraft had to fly, the smaller the bomb load it could carry. Normally the Spitfires carried two 250lb (113kg) bombs under the wings or a 500-pounder (226kg) under the fuselage. However, if the target was relatively close to base, the aircraft might carry the 500-pounder as well as two 250-pounders. Once the bombs had been dropped, the fighter could switch to the ground-attack role, its powerful armament making it an effective ground-strafing aircraft. When operating in the fighter-bomber role, Spitfires usually flew in sections of four or six, depending on the type of target and the weight of attack required.

Once the bombs had dropped, the fighter's powerful gun armament made it an effective ground-strafing aircraft

Flying Officer David Green fle Spitfires with No. 73 Squadron ov Italy and Yugoslavia during the fin months of the war. He describes th normal tactics for a dive-bombin attack in a Spitfire:

"Carrying two 250lb bombs, th Spitfire made a very fine dive-bombe It could attack accurately and didn need a fighter escort because as soon a the bombs had been released it wa a fighter. The briefing beforehan had to be good enough for us t be able to fly right up to the targe even if we had never been there befor identify it and bomb it. Becaus

AIR SUPPORT FOR THE ARMY, MORNING OF 10 NOVEMBER 1944

Squadron	Aircraft	Time up	Remarks
No. 7 SAAF	6 Spitfire	09.45	Bombed medium gun position
No. 1 SAAF	6 Spitfire	10.00	Bombed field guns near Forli
No. 601	6 Spitfire	10.15	Bombed field guns near Forli; light AA fire; one aircraft failed to pull out of dive possibly due to flak hit, pilot killed
No. 2 SAAF	6 Spitfire	10.20	Two aircraft returned early; rest bombed gun position and carried out strafing attacks; heavy AA from target, no losses
No. 92	6 Spitfire	10.25	Bombed gun positions S. Faenza
No. 92	6 Spitfire	10.30	Bombed and strafed gun and mortar positions near Faenza
No. 4 SAAF	6 Spitfire	10.40	Dive-bombed gun positions
No. 2 SAAF	6 Spitfire	11.05	Bombed 3 gun positions, target well strafed; light AA from target
No. 4 SAAF	6 Spitfire	11.35	Bombed gun positions

he flak was often accurate we didn't want to spend time circling in the target area before we went down to attack. We normally operated in sections of four, and would fly to the target at 10,000 feet in finger-four battle formation."

When the raiding force neared the target area, the Spitfires closed up and moved into loose echelon formation to starboard of the leader. David Green continued:

"As the target came into view I would position it so that it appeared to be running down the line of my port cannon. As the target disappeared under the wing, I would hold my heading. When the target emerged from under the trailing edge I would pull the aircraft up to kill the forward speed, roll it over on its back and let the nose drop until the target was lined up in the gunsight graticule. That way, one got the Spitfire to go down in the correct angle of dive of 60 degrees. It was a pretty steep dive, it felt as if one was going down vertically. The other aircraft in the section, Nos. 2, 3, and 4, would be following me down still in echelon."

When the leader's dive took him to an altitude of 4,000ft (1,219m) above the ground, he released his bombs.

"I would let go my bombs and call 'Bombs gone!'; the other chaps in the section would then release theirs. If there had been little or no flak the desire to see the results of the bombing was usually so

> "It was a pretty steep dive, it felt as if one was going down vertically."

great that I would pull hard on the stick to bring the aircraft out of the dive and into a slight climb, so that I could look over my shoulder to see where the bombs had gone. But if we were being fired at, we would use our high forward speed to get us down to ground level where there was cover."

During the final months of the war, almost every attack launched by the British army received strong fighter-bomber support. The example above shows the scale of air support for the British advance on the Montone River in Italy, on 10 November 1944. That morning, during a two-hour period, two RAF and four South African Air Force Spitfire squadrons flew 54 sorties to soften up the German defences. Air operations continued in the same vein throughout the rest of the day.

■ VERSATILITY ■

Given the ability of the Spitfire in the fighter-bomber role, the reader should remember that attacks on ground targets were far from everyone's thoughts when the Spitfire was conceived. As so often with this aircraft, it was a case of the very good basic design proving very good at a wide range of different roles.

The Spitfire remained in front-line service in the RAF for nearly a decade after the end of the war. In the next chapter, we shall observe the final stages of its lengthy career in that service and also in foreign air forces.

POST-WAR SPITFIRES

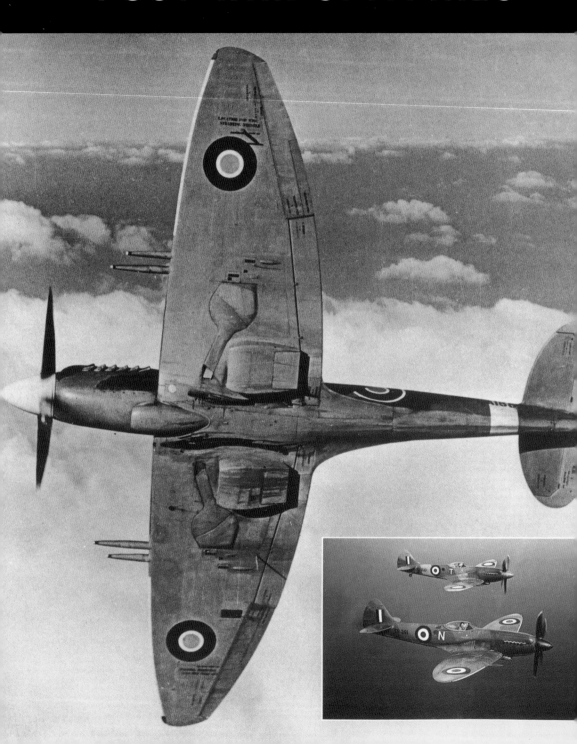

At the end of the war, just over 1,000 Spitfires were serving with RAF front-line units. About two-thirds of those were Mark Xs (or the essentially similar Mark XVIs). For a 'stop-gap' fighter put into production in a hurry, this had been a remarkably successful variant.

The Spitfire force was rapidly run down after the war as the RAF reduced its strength and many units converted to jet fighters. During the early post-war period, the Mark XVIII was the main fighter variant to equip fighter units in the Middle East and the Far East. Externally similar to the late production Mark XIV with bubble canopy and additional fuel tanks in the rear fuselage, this variant also featured a redesigned and strengthened wing. Production ran to some 300 aircraft, and the variant equipped six front-line squadrons.

The Mark XVIII saw action with Nos. 28 and 60 Squadrons in Malaya, engaging in bombing and strafing operations against Communist guerillas in that country. Serving in the Middle East with Nos. 32 and 208 Squadrons, this variant became involved in clashes during the Arab-Jewish conflict leading up to the establishment of the state of Israel.

As mentioned earlier, the Mark XXI had been intended as the 'definitive' fighter variant of the Spitfire. At the peak more than 1,800 were on order, but with the end of the war most of these were cancelled. In the event, production ended at 120 aircraft, and this variant served with only four front-line squadrons.

Main left: A Spitfire XXI tips its wing to show the revised wing shape of this and later variants. Note also the fairing doors covering the main wheels and the armament of four 20mm cannon introduced as standard with this version. *Above right:* After the war, Spitfires served in several second-line units. This Mark XVI operated with the Central Gunnery School. *Inset left and right:* Spitfire XVIIIs of No. 208 Squadron based at Fayid in the Suez Canal Zone in 1947.

SPITFIRE MARK XXII

Type Single-seat interceptor fighter

Armament Four Hispano 20mm cannon with 150 rounds each for the inner weapons and 175 rounds each for the outer weapons

Power plant One Rolls-Royce Griffon 61 liquid cooled V-12 engine with two-stage supercharger developing 2,035hp

Dimensions Span 36ft 1in (11.25m); length 32ft 11in (10.03m)

Weight Maximum loaded weight 10,086lb (4,574kg)

Performance Maximum speed 449mph at 25,000ft (723km/hr at 7,622m); service ceiling 45,500ft (13,872m)

Left: Mark XVIIIs of No. 28 Squadron pictured at Kai Tak, Hong Kong, late in 1950. The aircraft carries the black and white identification bands on the rear fuselage and above and below the wings, introduced soon after the start of the war in Korea.
Middle left: Spitfire made for two. After the war, small numbers of Spitfire XVIIIs and IXs were converted into two-seat trainers with dual controls. Trainer variants served with the Indian, Dutch, Egyptian and Irish air forces, though the type was not adopted by the RAF.
Below left: Spitfire PP139 served as a development prototype for the Mark XXI, and incorporated several new features. The enlarged fin with the straight leading edge and the windscreen with revised contours were not incorporated into production aircraft.

During the post-war period, the Mark XVIII was the main fighter variant to equip fighter units in the Middle East and Far East

The next major production fighter variant, the Spitfire XXII, was essentially a Mark XXI with a bubble canopy and the new enlarged tail assembly. The majority of Mark XXIIs went to Royal Auxiliary Air Force squadrons, reserve units manned by the so-called 'weekend pilots'. During 1948, 12 of the 20 RAuxAF squadrons re-equipped with Spitfire XXIIs.

■ FINAL VARIANT ■

The final Spitfire variant, the Mark XXIV, looked little different from the Mark XXII. Its main points of difference were two additional fuel tanks fitted in the rear fuselage, and wing fittings to carry six 60lb (27kg) rockets. Supermarine built 54 Mark XXIVs and converted 27 Mark XXIIs on the production line to this configuration. The final Mark XXIV, the last of more than 20,000 Spitfires built, left the factory at South Marston near Swindon in February 1948.

The majority of Mark XXIIs went to Royal Auxiliary Air Force squadrons

Only one front-line unit received the Spitfire XXIV, No. 80 Squadron based in Germany in January 1948. In July 1949, after the start of the Korean War, the unit moved to Hong Kong to provide air defence for the colony. The last RAF unit to operate Spitfires in the fighter role, it re-equipped with Hornets in January 1952. Photographic reconnaissance Mark XIXs continued in front-line service for a further two years, before this variant also ended its front-line career in the Far East. In April 1954, No. 81 Squadron in Malaya exchanged its trusty Spitfires for Meteors.

Although the Spitfire had passed out of front-line service, it would continue to perform second-line tasks in the RAF for three more years. The last full-time RAF unit to operate Spitfires was the civilian-manned Temperature and Humidity (THUM) Flight based at Woodvale in Lancashire. The unit's Mark XIXs, carrying meteorological measuring equipment, made daily flights to 30,000ft (9,144m) to record the weather conditions in each altitude band. These flights continued until June 1957, when the unit disbanded. Even then, the Spitfire's career in the RAF was not at an end. After the THUM Flight disbanded, one of its redundant Mark XIXs went to the Central Fighter Establishment at West Raynham to serve as a gate guardian. Service engineers lovingly maintained the aircraft in flying condition, however, and when the unit transferred to Binbrook, the Spitfire went too.

During 1963, Indonesia launched its claim to parts of Malayan territory, and threatened to use force to secure it. To meet the threat, the RAF sent reinforcements to the area, including detachments of Lightning fighters. The Indonesian Air Force operated Second World War Mustang fighters, and there was uncertainty on the best tactics for the Mach 2

Left and above: A few Spitfires were fitted with the contra-rotating propeller, comprising two three-bladed units rotating in opposite directions. Although this made the fighter easier to fly and a more steady gun platform, it came too late for general service use.

Above: The Mark XXII was similar to the Mark XXI, but featured a bubble canopy as well as a larger tailplane, fin and rudder.

fighters to engage these. To discover the answer, the CFE ran a combat trial using the Spitfire XIX as a stand-in for the Mustang. Mock combats between the two aircraft revealed that the older fighter stood little chance in a wartime encounter. The Lightning was almost invulnerable while it maintained high speed and did not enter a turning fight with the more nimble opponent. The best tactic for the Lightning was to position itself a few thousand feet below the piston-engined fighter, and make a steep climbing attack from there. This gave a good chance of getting into a missile-firing position on the Spitfire (or Mustang) without being seen. The trial at Binbrook took place

27 years after the maiden flight c the Spitfire, and probably represented th final warlike act in the aircraft's lon and distinguished career.

Also during the years following th Second World War, several foreign a forces operated Spitfires. The larges such operator was the French Ai Force, which took delivery of mor than 500 Mark Vs, VIIIs, IXs an XVIs. Some went to Vietnam and fle against Communist guerillas durin the initial stages of the long conflict i that country.

■ **SPITFIRES INTERNATIONAL** ▶

The Royal Dutch Air Force receive 76 Mark IXs, some of which saw com bat over what was then the Dutch Eas Indies. That conflict ran from 1947 t 1949, and ended with the foundatio of the modern state of Indonesia.

Other major post-war Spitfire use were the Turkish Air Force, whic received 273, the Royal Greek A Force with 242, and the Royal Belgia Air Force with 203. The Indian Air Forc received 159, the Italian Air Force 14(and the Czechoslovak Air Force 77.

Over a century has elapsed sinc Orville Wright made the first manne flight in a heavier-than-air flying machin In the turbulent history of militar aviation, no aircraft has carved a deepe niche than Mitchell's little fighter – whic somebody else chose to call 'Spitfire'.

Above: Spitfire XXIIs formed the main equipment of the Royal Auxiliary Air Force units during the late 1940s. These aircraft belonged to No. 613 (City of Manchester) Squadron based at Ringwood, which converted to the variant in the summer of 1948.
Left: Spitfire XXII of No. 607 (County of Durham) Squadron. The '4' painted on the fin, fuselage and wing was the aircraft's racing number for the Cooper Trophy air race in 1948.

Above: Mark IX of the Royal Dutch Air Force, which received 76 examples of this variant.
Left: From its external appearance, the final variant of the Spitfire, the Mark XXIV, was little different from the Mark XXII. The main changes were that it carried two additional fuel tanks in the rear fuselage, and wing fittings to carry six 60lb (27kg) rockets. Only No. 80 Squadron was equipped with this variant, and after a brief spell in Germany, the unit took its Mark XXIVs to Hong Kong.

Above: One of 77 examples of Mark IX passed to the Czechoslovak Air Force.
Left: The French Air Force was the largest foreign operator of Spitfires after the war, when that service took delivery of some 500 Mark Vs, VIIIs, IXs and XVIs.

Above: Three Spitfire PR Mark XIs of the Royal Norwegian Air Force, which also received 71 Mark IXs.
Left: The Italian Air Force received 140 Spitfire IXs after the war.
Right: Spitfire XIVs of the Royal Belgian Air Force, which received 134 examples of this variant, in addition to 69 Mark IXs and Mark XVIs.

Above and below: Partners in war, and also in peace. A Hurricane pictured with a Spitfire XIX of the Royal Air Force Battle of Britain Memorial Flight. These aircraft are firm favourites at present-day airshows.
Left: The Southern Rhodesian Air Force received 22 Spitfire XXIIs from surplus RAF stocks in 1951.

The main driving force for the development of the Spitfire came from the progressive increases in power from the Merlin, and later the Griffon, series of engines. In developing the extra power, the engines guzzled fuel faster, requiring larger capacity (and therefore heavier) fuel tanks to restore the fighter's range. Also, the more powerful engines required propellers with more blades to convert that rotational power into thrust. During its life, the Spitfire progressed from a two-bladed propeller to a three-blader, then to a four-blader, and finally to a five-bladed propeller. The greater the number of propeller blades, the greater the weight and also the greater the twisting forces they exerted on the airframe when the engine ran at full power. At the end of the fighter's career, it was necessary to fit an entirely new and larger tail assembly, to overcome these twisting forces.

Application of the hard-won lessons of air combat led to other problems. The RAF demanded the installation of armour to protect the pilot and vulnerable parts of the aircraft's structure, as well as additional equipment and more powerful (and therefore heavier) weaponry.

When the fighter sat on the ground, these increases in weight did not matter much, but in the stress of combat it was an entirely different matter. If the pilot pulled 6G in the turn, every part of the aircraft weighed six times as much. If the wings and the rest of the

THE PRICE OF SUCCESS

"I loved the Spitfire, in all of her many versions. But I have to admit that the later Marks, although they were faster than the earlier ones, were also much heavier and so did not handle so well. You did not have such positive control over them. One test of manoeuvrability was to throw the Spitfire into a flick roll and see how many times she rolled. With the Mark II or the Mark V one got two and a half flick rolls, but the Mark IX was heavier and you got only one and a half. With the later and still heavier versions one got even less.

"The essence of aircraft design is compromise, and an improvement at one end of the performance envelope is rarely achieved without a deterioration somewhere else."

ALEX HENSHAW, CHIEF TEST PILOT AT THE CASTLE BROMWICH SPITFIRE FACTORY

structure were not strong enough to withstand these increased forces, the airframe would be overstressed and weakened. In extreme cases, the structure might collapse altogether. So, to cope with each major increase in the fighter's weight, the airframe was continually being redesigned to increase its strength and maintain a safe load factor. In addition, and inevitably, each such redesign brought with it a further increase in weight. Thus, every improvement in performance, fire power, range or capability gave a further twist in the spiral of increased weight. And that in turn led to further deterioration in the fighter's handling characteristics.

5054	Prototype Spitfire, first flew in March 1936. Only one aircraft built.
Mark I	Similar to the prototype but with some revisions to the structure, this was the first production fighter version. The Mark I made its maiden flight in May 1938, and entered service in the following September.
Mark I Recon variants	Mark Is modified for the reconnaissance role, designated from IA to IG depending on the reconnaissance configuration of the cameras and fuel tanks carried. First such aircraft entered service in November 1939.
Mark II	Fighter version similar to the Mark I, but fitted with the more powerful Merlin 12 engine. Entered service in September 1940.
Mark III	Fighter version similar to the Mark I but with a redesigned internal structure and fitted with a retractable tail wheel. This variant did not go into production. In September 1941, the prototype Mark III served as a test bed for the Merlin 61 engine with two-stage supercharger.
Mark IV	Designation initially applied to the prototype Griffon-engined Spitfire. In 1941, the designation system was revised, and the Griffon aircraft became the Mark XX for a short time, before finally ending up as the Mark XII. The Mark IV designation was then re-allocated to reconnaissance versions.
Mark V	Fighter version similar to the Mark I, but fitted with the more powerful Merlin 45-series engine. The Mark V entered service in February 1941, and was built in very large numbers. It was the first variant to be fitted with bomb racks, and operated in the fighter-bomber role.
Mark VI	High-altitude interceptor fighter, similar to the Mark V but fitted with a pressurized cabin and longer-span wing. The Mark VI was built in small numbers and entered service in April 1942.
Mark VII	High-altitude interceptor fighter, similar to the Mark VI but powered by the Merlin 61-series engine with two-stage supercharger. Built in moderate numbers, the first squadron equipped with this variant became operational in April 1943.
Mark VIII	General-purpose fighter similar to the Mark VII but without the pressurized cabin. Entered service in the summer of 1943. Built in large numbers, all Mark VIIIs went to units based outside the United Kingdom. This variant also operated in the fighter-bomber role.
Mark IX	General-purpose fighter version based on the Mark V, but fitted with the Merlin 61-series engine. Entered service in June 1942. This variant was intended as a stop-gap, pending large-scale production of the Mark VIII. In the event, the Mark IX remained in production until the end of the war. With the externally similar Mark XVI, it was built in greater numbers than any other variant. Late-production aircraft were fitted with bubble canopies. This variant also operated in the fighter-bomber and fighter-reconnaissance roles.
Mark X	Photographic reconnaissance variant generally similar to the PR ID, but fitted with the Merlin 61-series engine and a pressurized cabin. Entered service in May 1944, and was built in small numbers.
Mark XI	Photographic reconnaissance variant similar to the Mark X but without the pressurized cabin. Entered service in December 1942, and became the most-used photographic reconnaissance variant.
Mark XII	Fighter version based on the Mark V but fitted with the early Griffon 2 engine with a single-stage supercharger. Originally it was designated the Mark IV, and then it was redesignated the Mark XX, before finally receiving this designation. Built in moderate numbers as a low-altitude fighter, all production aircraft had clipped wings. Entered service in February 1943.

Mark XIII   Low-altitude fighter-reconnaissance variant fitted with vertical and oblique cameras, and armed with four .303in (7.7mm) machine-guns. With only 26 examples produced, it entered service in the summer of 1943.

Mark XIV   Fighter version similar to the Mark VIII but fitted with the Griffon 61-series engine with two-stage supercharger. It entered service in February 1944. A fighter-reconnaissance version of the Mark XIV also appeared. The variant was built in large numbers, and the final production aircraft had bubble canopies.

Mark XV   Designation not applied to the Spitfire.

Mark XVI   Fighter version similar to the Mark IX but powered by the Merlin engine produced under licence by the American Packard Company. The two variants were produced side by side at the Castle Bromwich plant, and their external appearance was almost identical. The Mark XVI entered service in September 1944, and late-production aircraft were fitted with bubble canopies. This variant also operated in the fighter-bomber role.

Mark XVII   Designation not applied to the Spitfire.

Mark XVIII   Fighter-bomber version similar in external appearance to the late-model Mark XIV fitted with the bubble canopy, this variant featured a redesigned and strengthened wing, and carried additional fuel tanks in the rear fuselage. A fighter-reconnaissance version of the Mark XVIII also appeared. Built in moderate numbers after the war, it entered service in January 1947. All Mark XVIIIs went to units based outside the United Kingdom.

Mark XIX   Photographic reconnaissance variant which combined the Griffon 61 engine, the fuel tank layout of the Mark XI, and a pressurized cabin that was a marked improvement over that fitted to the Mark X. It entered service in the summer of 1944, and became the most-used reconnaissance variant during the final year of the war. The Mark XIX remained in front-line service in the RAF until 1954.

Mark XX   Designation applied to the prototype Griffon-powered Spitfire, alias the Mark IV, following the re-allocation of Mark numbers. After a further re-allocation of Mark numbers, this aircraft was redesignated as a Mark XII, and the Mark XX designation fell vacant.

Mark XXI   Fighter version with a redesigned and strengthened wing and fuselage, fitted with the Griffon 61-series engine. The Mark XXI entered service in April 1945, and saw some action before the war ended. Following the end of the conflict, several large contracts for the Mark XXI were cancelled, and the variant was built in only moderate numbers.

Mark XXII   Fighter version similar to the Mark XXI, but with a bubble canopy. Production aircraft fitted with enlarged tailplane, fin and rudder. The Mark XXII entered service in November 1947, and became the main post-war production variant. It remained in service with Royal Auxiliary Air Force squadrons until March 1951.

Mark XXIII   A projected fighter version that was to have been fitted with laminar-flow wing; not built.

Mark XXIV   Fighter version based on the Mark XXII, but with two additional fuel tanks in the rear fuselage and wing fittings to carry six 60lb (27kg) rockets. Only one squadron operated this variant. The type remained in front-line service in the RAF until January 1952.

ABOUT THE AUTHOR

Dr Alfred Price served as an aircrew officer in the Royal Air Force and, during a flying career spanning 15 years, he logged some 4,000 flying hours. While in the RAF he specialized and instructed in electronic warfare and airfreighting tactics. He subsequently became a full-time aviation historian and writer, and is acknowledged as a world authority on the Spitfire. He has written more than 40 books on aviation subjects, including co-authoring *Haynes Manuals* on the Supermarine Spitfire and Avro Vulcan, and has often been asked to compile aviation questions for the BBC television show *Mastermind*. Dr Price holds a PhD in History, and is a fellow of the Royal Historical Society.